Student's CD-ROM

Track	Module/lesson	Content
1	Titles	
2	1a	Read
3	1b	Read
4	Culture page 1	
5	2a	Read
6	2b	Read
7	Song 1	
8	3b	Read
9	Culture page 2	
10	4a	Read
11	4b	Read
12	Song 2	
13	5a	Read
14	5b	Read
15	Culture page 3	
16	6a	Read
17	Song 3	
18	7a	Read
19	7b	Read
20	Culture page 4	
21	8a	Read
22	8b	Read
23	Song 4	

Student's audio CD track list

Track	Module/lesson	Content
1	Titles	
2	1a	Read
3	1b	Read
4	2a	Read
5	2b	Read
6	Song 1	
7	3b	Read
8	4a	Read
9	4b	Read
10	Song 2	
11	5a	Read
12	5b	Read
13	6a	Read
14	Song 3	
15	7a	Read
16	7b	Read
17	8a	Read
18	8b	Read
19	Song 4	

Contents

Module 1 **Let's chat** 4

Module 2 **Ready for anything** 14

Module 3 **Buy it!** 25

Module 4 **Being a teen** 35

Module 5 **Globetrotting** 45

Module 6 **Time out** 56

Module 7 **Mother nature** 67

Module 8 **Image** 78

Student's Book pp. 6-7

A. Complete the sentences and find the word in the purple boxes.

1. My computer got a _____ but luckily I got rid of it before it caused any serious damage.
2. Let me _____ you to our new colleague, Alex.
3. That's the new _____ game my brother bought yesterday.
4. How many _____ has this social networking site got?
5. It's a good idea to _____ our product online. That way more people can see it.
6. You can't _____ what a mess the house was in after the get-together.
7. Tom is a _____ of the new sports club.
8. For more information about the company, you can visit our _____.

1. V I R U S
2. I N T R O D U C E
3. V I R T U A L
4. U S E R S
5. A D V E R T I S E
6. I M A G I N E
7. M E M B E R
8. W E B S I T E

The word in the purple boxes is: _____

B. Choose a, b or c.

Hi Nora,
I hope you are well because I'm not. I'm having problems with Francis and I really need your advice. You know how she tends (1) __to__ lie sometimes. Well, the (2) __other__ day, some friends had a small get-together. I couldn't go but Francis really wanted to. She told me that she would lie to her parents so she could go and of course I (3) __disagreed__ with the idea. In the end, she told her parents that she would be at my house and went to the get-together. Francis sent me an SMS explaining everything but it (4) __seems__ that I never got it. The next day I sent her a message asking her if she had had a good time. Her brother saw it and told their parents. The final (5) __straw__ was when her mother called me and started asking me questions. It was quite (6) __embarrasing__ because I didn't know what to say and she realised something was up. Francis got in trouble and now she isn't talking to me. Also, I've heard that she's saying some (7) __nasty__ things about me. Imagine that! It's not like I (8) __committed__ a crime. And anyway, it's not my fault she lied to her parents. What should I do?
Mary

1. a. into   b. to   c. for
2. a. next   b. other   c. some
3. a. complained   b. pretended   c. disagreed
4. a. sounds   b. seems   c. looks
5. a. drawback   b. stone   c. straw
6. a. embarrassing   b. amusing   c. embarrassed
7. a. useful   b. nasty   c. useless
8. a. made   b. did   c. committed

C. Circle the correct words.

1. **A:** Jim visits / ~~is visiting~~ New York this summer.
   B: Wow that ~~sounds~~ / is sounding great!
2. **A:** I can't stand Peter. He always tell / ~~is always telling~~ me what to do!
   B: I ~~know~~ / am knowing. He's so bossy.
3. **A:** The *Rovers* are the best football team.
   B: I ~~don't think~~ / 'm not thinking so.
   A: What do you talk / ~~are you talking~~ about? They're brilliant.
4. **A:** Do you come / ~~Are you coming~~ to the theatre with us tonight?
   B: What time ~~does the play start~~ / the play is starting?
   A: At six o'clock.
   B: I'm afraid I can't. My lessons don't finish / ~~aren't finishing~~ till eight.
5. **A:** I didn't know you still live / ~~are living~~ with your parents.
   B: I don't. I stay / ~~am staying~~ with them for a few weeks, till I find another flat.

D. Complete the text with the Present Simple or the Present Progressive of the verbs in brackets.

Hey Peter,

How's it going? I (1) __am writing__ (write) to ask for your help. I (2) __hope__ (hope) that you (3) __do not mind__ (not mind). This week I (4) __am moving__ (move) out of the bedroom I shared with my brother and I (5) __am getting__ (get) my own room. It's small but it's got a big window and I (6) __like__ (like) it. Anyway, my problem is the colours. My dad (7) __is planing__ (plan) to paint it tomorrow, so I (8) __need__ (need) to choose the colours today. I (9) __love__ (love) the way you've painted your bedroom in two colours but I (10) __don't know__ (not know) what to choose for mine. As you know, I (11) __spend__ (spend) quite a lot of time in my room so I (12) __want__ (want) it to be really nice. Any ideas? I (13) __am thinking__ (think) of surfing the Net to find a website about bedroom decorating. (14) __Do you know__ (you / know) of any sites I can check out? My sister (15) __usually helps__ (usually / help) me out with Internet research, but these days she (16) __is studying__ (study) all the time and hasn't got the time. So, can you help me out?

Write back asap,

Kevin

▶▶ Student's Book pp. 8-9

A. Complete the sentences with the words in the box. There are two extra words which you do not need to use.

| paste | download | install | attach | click | print | delete | scroll |

1. I've found a new website where you can _____ lots of songs from.
2. _____ on the image you want twice.
3. Make sure you _____ the photos from our holiday to the e-mail.
4. Select the web address. Then copy and _____ it into the address bar.
5. Oh no! Did you just _____ everything? It took me hours to finish that project.
6. When the website opens _____ down the page until you see the red button.

1a

B. Complete the text with the comparative or superlative form of the adjectives or adverbs in brackets.

ESPERANTO "Saluton!*"
(* Saluton = hello in Esperanto)

In the late 19th century, a man named L.L. Zamenhof created a completely new language that he hoped would be the (1) _exciting_ (exciting) development in the history of languages. He called this language 'Esperanto' and it was designed to be (2) _easier_ (easy) to learn than any other language, with the basic rules taking only a few days to understand. He hoped it would become the (3) _most popular_ (popular) second language in the world. But to his disappointment, it did not become as (4) _popular_ (popular) as he expected. Zamenhof believed that the world would become a (5) _better_ (good) and (6) _more peaceful_ (peaceful) place with a single, common language. He thought everyone would feel (7) _closer_ (close) to each other if they were no longer divided by different languages. No one knows exactly how many people speak Esperanto fluently, but there may be between 10,000 to (8) _more_ (many) than 1.5 million people. Traditional languages such as English may be (9) _harder_ (hard) to learn but they continue to be the (10) _most common_ (common) second languages for students all over the world.

C. Complete the second sentence so that it has a similar meaning to the first sentence, using the word given. Do not change the word given. You must use between two and five words including the word given.

1. If you keep practising, it'll become easy for you. **more**

   The _more you practice, the easier_ it'll become for you.

2. Sandra receives more e-mails than Kate. **as**

   Kate doesn't receive _as many e-mails as_ Sandra.

3. Your younger sister is becoming quite tall. **and**

   Your younger sister is getting _quite taller and taller_.

4. If you run faster, you'll get to school quicker. **the**

   The faster _you run, the quicker_ you'll get to school.

5. Ben is not as interested in reading as his brother. **less**

   Ben is _not as keen on reading as_ his brother.

6. Lisa's hair is a lot longer than Helen's. **much**

   Lisa's hair _is longer_ than Helen's.

D. Complete the dialogues with the phrases a-g. There are two extra phrases which you do not need to use.

a. turned it on
b. shut it down now
c. drop him a line
d. have a word with
e. give them a call
f. call me back
g. kept in touch with

1. **Matthew** My computer isn't working. Can you help me, Steve?
   Steve Have you (1) _a_ ? I can't see any lights on anywhere.
   Matthew I'm not that silly! The problem is that I can't hear anything.
   Steve Oh, that's never happened to me before. Look, here's the number for technical support. Why don't you (2) _e_ ?
   Matthew I did and I am waiting for them to (3) _f_ .

2. **Sam** Hi, Jess. Did you get my e-mail about the get-together?
   Jess Yeah, thanks. I need to (4) _d_ my parents about it first, but I think I'll come.
   Sam That's great news! Tell your cousin about it, too.
   Jess He's at university now so I'll send him an e-mail.
   Sam OK great. Can you give me his address? I'll (5) _c_ to give him directions to my house.
   Jess Sure, no problem.

Student's Book pp. 10-11

A. Complete the sentences with the correct prepositions.

1. I'm sick __of__ her behaviour. She is always rude to me.
2. Kate is bored __of__ her life in Brighton. She wants to move to another city.
3. You don't seem very enthusiastic __about__ the game.
4. Mandy is interested __in__ learning a foreign language.
5. I'm keen __on__ playing tennis. I play three times a week.
6. Most teenage boys are fond __of__ football.
7. Jack is fed __up__ with waiting, so he is leaving.
8. I'm tired __of__ watching TV. Let's go for a walk.

B. Complete the sentences with the words in the box. There are two extra words which you do not need to use.

~~lonely~~   ~~creative~~   earn   ~~entertaining~~   ~~improve~~   teamwork   socialise   ~~suppose~~

1. How much do you __earn__, if you don't mind me asking?
2. She is so __creative__. I could never make my own accessories.
3. I __suppose__ you're right. It's too windy to go sailing.
4. We need to __improve__ our school's facilities.
5. This TV programme is much more __entertaining__ than the one we were watching before.
6. I moved to a new neighbourhood so I get __lonely__ sometimes.

C. Here are some sentences about Peter's new job at a company. Complete the second sentence so that it means the same as the first. Use no more than three words.

1. Peter loves his new job.
   Peter is crazy __about__ his new job.
2. Peter's previous job was more challenging than his new one.
   Peter's new job isn't __as challenging as__ his previous one.
3. Peter likes his job as well as the people he works with.
   Apart __from__ his job, Peter also likes the people he works with.
4. Peter is improving at his work.
   Peter is getting __better__ at his work.
5. Peter's friend, Gloria, admires his work a lot.
   Peter's friend, Gloria, is a big fan __of__ his work.

D. Join the sentences using and, but, or, so or because.

1. My friend Harry loves basketball. We always play in our free time.
   ... basketball, so we ...
2. Jane and her friends sometimes hang out at the park. They sometimes hang out at the shopping centre.
   ... at the park, but they ...
3. I'm very upset. I lost a very important match yesterday.
   __because__
4. I don't like Carrie. She's always talking about herself.
   __because__
5. Mary usually works part-time. Today she is working full-time.
   __but__

▶▶ Student's Book pp. 12-13

A. Circle the correct words.

1. Only time will **tell** / say if the business will be successful.
2. Ron bought a new **portable** / flexible hard disk drive where he can store up to 500GB.
3. One of the most important technological introductions / **inventions** of the 20th century is the computer.
4. Your mobile phone has got a wide ability / **variety** of ringtones, but you always choose the most awful ones.
5. Does the price provide / **include** tax?
6. You usually cannot use your mobile phone in lifts since there is a **weak** / wide signal.
7. Amanda came in / **up** with a wonderful idea for our Science project.
8. My new mobile has got a 2GB memory card so I can **store** / invent a lot of data.
9. Pete couldn't make any phone calls because he had a weak browser / **signal**.
10. I can't stand that **ringtone** / feature. It's so annoying. Please change it.

B. Complete the dialogue with the Past Simple of the verbs in brackets.

Marion Hi, Ken. Wow! I (1) _didn't know_ (not know) you
(2) _had_ (have) a new laptop.
Ken I (3) _bought_ (buy) it last Friday.
Marion It looks pretty cool.
Ken Thanks.
Marion What's wrong? You don't look very excited about it.
Ken Well yesterday, I (4) _decided_ (decide) to download the latest software updates for it. So, I (5) _searched_ (search) the Internet and (6) _found_ (find) all the software I (7) _needed_ (need).
Marion (8) _Did you install_ (you / install) it?
Ken Yes, and that's when my nightmare (9) _started_ (start)! Now my laptop is full of viruses.
Marion No way! (10) _did you call_ (you / call) the Customer Service Department?
Ken Well, unfortunately they (11) _weren't_ (not be) very helpful so now I don't know what to do.
Marion Oh no.

C. Rewrite each of the words or phrases in bold using *used to*.

1. When I was younger, I **didn't like** hanging out at the shopping centre, but now I do. _____
2. In the past mobile phones **didn't have** many features, but now they do. _____
3. As a teenager, Peter **bought** expensive gadgets all the time, but now he doesn't. _____
4. **Did you download** all the latest updates for your smartphone as a teenager? _____
5. When I was at university, I **drank** coffee at all hours, but now I only have some in the morning. _____

D. Complete the sentences with the correct form of *used to, get used to* or *be used to* and circle the correct word after each blank.

1. I _____ **like / liking** playing computer games with my friend, Tom, because he always won. It was really annoying. Now I _____ **lose / losing**, so I don't mind any more.

2. I _____ **use / using** a computer because I've had one since I was five. In the past, I _____ **do / doing** everything on my computer, even keep in touch with friends through SN sites. Now I prefer not to use my computer to communicate with friends. We meet up and do things together instead.

3. I _____ **like / liking** searching the Internet for information because it was difficult and confusing. As I got older, I _____ **use / using** it and now I think it's the best way to do research.

▶▶ Student's Book pp. 14-15

A. Complete the dialogue with the words in the box. There are two extra words which you do not need to use.

| complaining | ~~explain~~ | ~~mention~~ | ~~gossiping~~ | ~~yell~~ | ~~argue~~ | ~~discuss~~ | chat |

Rita Hi, Jenny. Listen, I was chatting with some girls from school today.
Jenny Yeah, and?
Rita Well, they were (1) _gossiping_ about you.
Jenny What!? What were they saying?
Rita OK, OK, don't (2) _yell_ at me. I just wanted to (3) _mention_ it to you.
Jenny So, what did they say?
Rita Well, they were talking about the way you dress.
Jenny What's wrong with it?

Rita Your clothes are quite different. You can't (4) _argue_ with them about that.
Jenny I suppose so. But I've just got my own personal style, that's all.
Rita That's what I tried to (5) _explain_ to them.
Jenny This isn't the first time you know!
Rita Calm down. Let's (6) _discuss_ the situation and maybe we'll find a solution.
Jenny OK.

B. Complete the text with the correct form of the words in capitals.

4G Technology

The (1) _____ of the arrival of 4G phones meant great news for technology fans. Also known as Fourth- (2) _____ Communications System, 4G is a term used to describe the latest step in wireless (3) _____.

The (4) _____ of the 4G system made voice, data and streaming multimedia available to users anytime, anywhere. Suddenly phones could compete with laptops as a convenient means of getting (5) _____ and (6) _____. The 4G system provides top quality and high security. It is definitely an (7) _____ on 3G models.

(8) _____ to the Internet is also much faster. In fact, it's as much as 10 times faster than with 3G phones. This is an important (9) _____ and gadget enthusiasts all want their own 4G phone. However, with technological (10) _____ taking place so incredibly fast, people are already waiting for the next gadget to take over the market!

ANNOUNCE
GENERATE

COMMUNICATE
INVENT

INFORM
ENTERTAIN
IMPROVE
CONNECT
ACHIEVE

DEVELOP

1b

C. Choose a, b, c or d.

In the past, I (1) **used** [didn't] to enjoy talking on the phone very much. Actually, I hated it so I avoided it. My children and grandchildren (2) **used** to ring me all the time and (3) **discuss** about this. I told them that I preferred speaking to people in person. It always annoyed me that I couldn't see the person I was talking to. Anyway, I was (4) **chatting** with my grandson the other day and he (5) **mentioned** video calling over the Internet. It seems that everyone is doing it these days. He spoke with my other grandchildren and they came up with a great idea. They bought me a laptop. Then my youngest grandson came round my house and (6) **helped** me download a program and then set it up. And that was it! Now, I communicate with them all the time, and they are very happy. You can tell from the (7) **expression** on their faces. It's also very (8) **convenient** because it doesn't take (9) **along** a lot of room, so I can put it anywhere in the house. Sometimes I even talk to them while I'm in the kitchen cooking! More importantly, I haven't had another (10) **argument** with my family about not keeping in touch.

1. **a. used** b. wasn't used c. didn't use d. use
2. a. didn't use **b. used** c. use d. did use
3. **a. complain** **b. discuss** c. yell d. argue
4. a. explaining b. complaining c. mentioning d. chatting
5. a. gossiped **b. mentioned** c. argued d. explained
6. a. used to help b. was helped **c. helped** d. got used to helping
7. a. decision **b. expression** c. imagination d. discussion
8. a. light b. powerful **c. convenient** d. comfortable
9. a. on **b. up** c. off **d. along**
10. a. explanation b. improvement c. creation **d. argument**

▶▶ Student's Book pp. 16-17

A. Circle the correct words.

Sandra Welcome to the party, Charlie. I'm **glad** / proud you came.

Charlie Thanks Sandra. I wouldn't have refused / **missed** it for the world.

Sandra I hope you enjoy yourself. It will be a great **moment** / **opportunity** for you to make some new friends.

Charlie Though / **Absolutely**, I've been looking forward to it all week.

Sandra Come and meet Johnny. He is **hilarious** / ridiculous. He always tells the best jokes.

Becky Hi, Anna. How are you happening / **keeping**?

Anna I'm OK, but I am very angry with my sister. She has really let me **down** / away.

Becky Why, what happened?

Anna She's been meaning / **nagging** me for ages to take her to the cinema, so I bought the tickets but she arrived an hour late and we missed the film.

Becky Oh, I see. Well, do you want to come with me to see the next film at 8 o'clock?

Anna That sounds great. Thanks, Becky. Bring / **Count** me in!

Becky Bring your sister **along** / with, too. Don't be angry with her.

B. Read the situations and reply to the notes made.

1. Lisa and I are going to the skating rink tomorrow. How about coming along?
   — a. no / look after sister
   — b. absolutely

   a. _____
   b. _____

2. We're going to the shopping centre on Saturday, do you feel like coming along?
   — a. sure
   — b. sorry / can't

   a. _____
   b. _____

3. I won the school swimming competition! — fantastic

   _____

4. Do you want to come to the park with us to play football?
   — a. can't / finish homework
   — b. of course

   a. _____
   b. _____

C. Use the sentences/phrases to complete the e-mail. There are two extra which you do not need to use.

a. Give my regards to everyone
b. Take care
c. Well, that's all for now
d. I couldn't believe it when I read that
e. How could I say no
f. I know it's taken me ages to reply, but
g. I'm writing to let you know
h. Let me fill you in
i. Thanks for inviting me to the wedding

Dear Harry,

Hi! Thanks for your e-mail. **(1)** _____ I've been so busy with exams at school. **(2)** _____ your brother is getting married! That's fantastic news! Your whole family must be really excited.

(3) _____. I'm definitely coming. **(4)** _____? I love big family get-togethers! They are wonderful opportunities for everyone to see each other and enjoy themselves. So, what else are you up to? Are you very busy helping out with the preparations?

Now that we are talking about family news, I have some of my own. **(5)** _____. My sister Fay's been accepted into Oxford University! She did really well in her exams and will start studying there next September. My parents are so proud.

So, I guess we've both got good news at the moment! Anyway, I have to get back to studying now. **(6)** _____. I'll see you all at the wedding. I know you are very busy now, but try to keep in touch.

(7) _____,
Chris

D. Read the e-mail again and match the paragraphs 1-4 with the topics a-d.

Paragraph 1 ◯   a. Chris asks Harry to say hello to someone and write back.
Paragraph 2 ◯   b. Chris talks about his news.
Paragraph 3 ◯   c. Chris says hello and gives his reason for not writing sooner.
Paragraph 4 ◯   d. Chris accepts his invitation and asks Harry about his news.

11

1 Round-up

A. Complete the blanks in the text with one word.

Film-making Tips!

Are you crazy (1) _____ the cinema? Would you like to make your own short film but believe that you can't? Well, producing a simple film isn't (2) _____ difficult as you think. Here are some useful tips to get you started.

First of all, you need a good plot. You can use real-life stories or just your imagination. If you don't have any ideas, then give your friends (3) _____ call, sit down all together and start writing. I'm sure you'll come (4) _____ with something. Friends can also be used as actors. Even if they aren't (5) _____ to acting, they'll do well with some good instructions. I'm sure they won't let you (6) _____!

Apart (7) _____ the plot and the actors, you must also find costumes, make-up and decoration for the scenes. (8) _____ cheapest solution is to use your own things or make things. All you have to do is get creative. You can also get ideas from sources such (9) _____ the Internet or books.

So, don't waste any more time. If you are interested (10) _____ film-making, get a camera and start filming. (11) _____ the way, the more you practise, the (12) _____ experienced you get and the better your films will become. Good luck!

B. Choose a, b, c or d.

1. Helen is very enthusiastic _____ meeting her new classmates.
   a. to   b. about
   c. with   d. for

2. Why did you _____ down the laptop? I was using it!
   a. turn   b. close
   c. shut   d. press

3. You can just drop me a _____ when you decide the time of our meeting.
   a. message   b. line
   c. word   d. call

4. Before you use your new mobile for the first time, you should _____ it for at least 5 hours.
   a. charge   b. restart
   c. upload   d. install

5. _____ down to the end of the website. That's where the pictures are.
   a. Select   b. Scroll
   c. Click   d. Press

6. If you don't know, let me fill you _____.
   a. up   b. on
   c. in   d. out

7. When Dad comes home, he wants to _____ a word with you.
   a. say   b. give
   c. receive   d. have

8. I think you owe me a(n) _____ for your behaviour.
   a. argument   b. discussion
   c. decision   d. explanation

C. Choose a, b, c or d.

1. He _____ Spanish but his wife doesn't.
   a. speaks   b. spoke
   c. is speaking   d. used to speak

2. Pam _____ with her sister till her house is painted.
   a. stays   b. stayed
   c. is staying   d. is used to staying

3. I'm _____ to working early in the morning, so I'm always late for work.
   a. not used   b. used
   c. got used   d. was used

4. This programme _____ interesting as I thought.
   a. is more   b. is less
   c. isn't as   d. is the most

5. Gary is _____ than Andrew.
   a. as chubby   b. chubby
   c. a lot chubbier d. the chubbiest

6. You _____ to the weather in London, so don't worry.
   a. will get used   b. are being used
   c. got used   d. use to

12

D. Look at the texts. What does each one say? Choose a, b or c.

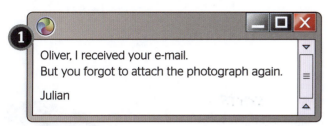

1. Oliver, I received your e-mail.
But you forgot to attach the photograph again.
Julian

a. Oliver didn't remember to send a photograph with the e-mail.
b. Julian sent an e-mail to Oliver with a photograph.
c. Julian has been meaning to send Oliver a photograph.

2. Hi Emma,
Sorry about my last text. I can't get used to the buttons on my new mobile. Anyway, count me in! I won't let you down.
Isabel

a. Isabel refused Emma's invitation.
b. Isabel hasn't decided what she's going to do yet.
c. Isabel accepted Emma's invitation.

3. If you require any assistance, press the button and a nurse will be with you immediately.

Press the button
a. when the nurse comes to you.
b. if the nurse does not come immediately.
c. when you need help from a nurse.

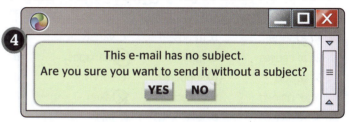

4. This e-mail has no subject.
Are you sure you want to send it without a subject?
YES   NO

a. You should click NO if you want to send the e-mail without a subject.
b. You don't have to write a subject before you send the e-mail.
c. You need to write a different subject from the one you have entered.

5. Tanya,
Josie called. She's found a less expensive computer for you. However, it means having to buy an antivirus program. Call her back by tomorrow if you want her to order it for you.
Dad

a. Tanya's friend found her a cheaper antivirus program.
b. Tanya will have to pay extra for an antivirus program.
c. Tanya has to contact Josie if she doesn't want to buy the antivirus program.

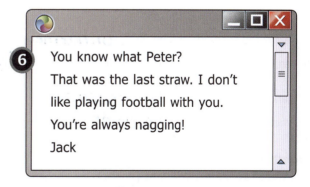

6. You know what Peter?
That was the last straw. I don't like playing football with you. You're always nagging!
Jack

a. Jack is bored of playing football.
b. Jack and Peter are always complaining about football.
c. Jack is fed up with Peter's behaviour.

2a

Student's Book pp. 20-21

A. Choose a, b, c or d.

Since 1980, the Make-A-Wish Foundation has been helping children with all (1) **sorts** of serious illnesses by making their wishes come true. The foundation, with offices in over 36 countries, tries hard to bring happiness to as many children as possible. In the US, it (2) **manages** to make a child's wish come true every 40 minutes. Fortunately, there are about 25,000 volunteers who (3) **support** its work and help it succeed.

The foundation has (4) **taken** my school's attention, too. So we're organising a festival to (5) **raise** some money and make a (6) **donation**. The festival is on 15th March, at 6pm. It will include a theatrical performance, music and snacks. It will be open to the (7) **public**, so you can bring friends and family if you want.

Let's all get together for this (8) **cause** and help make a difference in the world!

1. **a.** sorts   b. trends   c. variety   d. styles
2. a. causes   b. gets   **c.** manages   d. tends
3. a. add   **b.** support   c. survive   d. persuade
4. **a.** gained   b. collected   c. taken   d. made
5. a. give   b. take   **c.** raise   d. add
6. a. gift   b. challenge   **c.** donation   d. task
7. a. people   **b.** public   c. society   d. elderly
8. a. competition   **b.** cause   c. attention   d. task

B. Complete the dialogues with the words in the box. There are two extra words which you do not need to use.

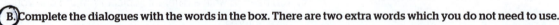

~~injured~~   survived   ~~unusual~~   ~~skydiving~~   ~~persuade~~   ~~unharmed~~   ~~brave~~   hanging

1. **A:** Have you ever tried (1) **skydiving**? It's so cool!
   B: No, I haven't. I'm not as (2) **brave** as you are.

2. **A:** A university caught fire yesterday.
   B: Really? Did everyone escape (3) **unharmed** from the burning building?
   A: Yes. But unfortunately one of the firefighters was (4) **injured**.

3. **A:** Mark always tries the most (5) **unusual** sports. Last weekend, he went zorbing.
   B: I know. He tried to (6) **persuade** me to go with him but I refused.

C. Circle the correct words.

1. Can you please turn on the **light** / **lights** in the kitchen and the living room?
2. John wants to spend more **times** / **time** with his wife and children.
3. We need some **wood** / **woods** for the fire.
4. All of Sally's clothes **are** / **is** trendy.
5. My mum has only got 3 grey **hair** / **hairs**.
6. This furniture **are** / **is** very old.
7. Plenty of **light** / **lights** comes into the room from the window.
8. Don't stand out in the **rain** / **rains**. Come inside.

D. Choose a, b, c or d.

1. **A:** How *much* sugar do you want in your coffee?
   B: Just a teaspoon.
   a. many   b. much   c. little   d. few

2. We need to buy some pencils. There are only *a few* left.
   a. little   b. a little   c. a few   d. few

3. Can I borrow *some* paper for my printer?
   a. some   b. much   c. little   d. plenty

4. There's very *little* butter in the cake, so it's healthier than you think.
   a. few   b. a few   c. a little   d. little

5. He's always got ~~a lot~~ *lots of* work to do at the weekend.
   a. a lot   **b.** lots of   c. lot   d. lots

6. You don't need to cook. There is *plenty of* food left from yesterday.
   a. plenty of   b. lots   c. a few   d. much

7. Alice is lonely. She seems to have *very* few friends here.
   a. very   b. too   c. not many   d. only

8. Linda has got *no* money with her, so I'll pay for both of us.
   a. a little   b. no   c. few   d. any

9. Don't worry. There isn't *any* change in our plans.
   a. some   b. few   c. any   d. no

10. **A:** Do you enjoy going to concerts?
    B: Yes, I like them *a lot*.
    a. many   b. very   c. much   d. a lot

▶▶ Student's Book pp. 22-23

A. Complete the sentences using *in* or *out of* and the words in the box.

| the question | order | trouble | shape | a bad mood | particular | common | a hurry | danger | case |

1. I was _____, so I took a taxi to get to work.

2. **A:** Dad, could I go out with my friends tonight?
   B: It's Monday today, so it's _____. Maybe some other time.

3. I'm really _____. I haven't been to the gym for months.

4. Tina and Penny are twins but they don't really have much _____.

5. The coffee machine is _____. We need to buy a new one.

6. He drove so fast that I really felt my life was _____.

7. Diana is _____ today. Let's ask her why.

8. Do you know what to do _____ of fire?

9. I don't have a problem with your cat _____. It's just that I don't like cats in general.

10. The boys broke the neighbour's window while they were playing football and they got _____.

B. Circle the correct words.

1. The money will go to those who are most in **need** / needs.
2. He isn't ancient / **mature** enough to get married and start a family.
3. Andrew has **gained** / earned weight recently.
4. Fay slipped and fell on the land / **ground**.
5. How much is the membership tip / **fee** for the new gym on Maple Street?
6. Unfortunately, I didn't succeed / **manage** to finish my project on time.
7. Monica made a tie / **donation** to a charity last week.

C. Complete the sentences with the correct relative pronoun/adverb. If they can be omitted, put them in brackets.

1. Joanne is the girl _who_ won the swimming race last week.
2. This is the place _where_ our parents first met.
3. That's the smartphone _that_ my brother wants to buy.
4. There's the guy _who_ sister lives next door.
5. The strawberries, ~~that~~ _which_ were in the fridge, were delicious. I ate them all.
6. That's the boy _that_ I was talking to you about the other day.
7. Susan, _who_ speaks Italian very well, is Nora's cousin.
8. The house, _in which_ Harry used to live, had a beautiful garden.

D. Join the sentences below using non-defining relative clauses.

1. There is an important football match on television tomorrow. I don't want to miss it.

   There is an important football match on the TV, that I don't want to miss.

2. William is moving next week. We're having a going-away party for him.

   who

3. We had dinner at Le Cirque. Lots of famous people eat there.

   where

4. Vivian's sister is a talented singer. She visited us yesterday.

   _____

E. Join the sentences below using relative pronouns or relative adverbs, adding commas where necessary. Make any other necessary changes.

1. We stayed at a hotel last summer. It was a very nice hotel.

   The hotel _at which we stayed last summer was very nice._

2. Sam's father is a famous writer. Sam is one of my best friends.

   Sam _is my best friend whos father is a writer_

3. Tom wrote two books. They became best-sellers.

   The two books _that Tom wrote became best-sellers._

4. Our aunt lives in Lisbon. She does a lot of charity work for the homeless.

   Our aunt _that does alot of charity... lives in_ ~~London~~ _Lisbon_

Student's Book pp. 24-25

A. Complete the text with the words in the box. There are two extra words which you do not need to use.

strict   instance   ambitious   patient   courageous   passionate   fact   intelligent   respect   extremely

My favourite teacher at school is my History teacher, Mr Mills. He's (1) _____ popular with all the students. He's sometimes (2) _____ with us, especially about things like homework and being late for class. For (3) _____ , he doesn't let us in if we are late. However, he's always got lots of energy in the classroom and you can see that he's (4) _____ about his job. He's also very (5) _____ and he takes his time helping each student. We all really (6) _____ him and behave well during his classes. In addition, he must be very (7) _____ because he always knows the answers to our questions. I really admire him as a teacher. In (8) _____ , I wish all of my teachers were more like him.

B. Choose a, b, c or d.

A: Hey, Sam. There's an advertisement in the newspaper for the job of a (1) _____ in a hotel. Do you think I can work there?

B: Sure you can. You speak three languages. You can use a computer well and you are very (2) _____. That's what they are looking for.

A: Yes, but it also says they would like someone who can work well (3) _____ pressure and I am not so sure about that.

B: What do you mean? I think you deal (4) _____ difficult situations really well. You are perfect for the job!

A: Thanks for being so (5) _____ Sam, I think I will go for it!

1. a. paramedic   **b. receptionist**   c. model   d. businessman
2. a. unselfish   b. weird   **c. responsible**   d. stressful
3. a. in   b. on   **c. under**   d. over
4. **a. with**   b. to   c. on   d. for
5. a. reliable   b. sociable   c. dedicated   **d. encouraging**

A: Hi, Anna. Did you hear about my cousin, Brad? He won a reward for his service to the (1) _____ as a policeman.

B: That's great. He deserves it. He is very (2) _____ so it's great news that he's won a prize.

A: Yes. He's someone that everyone (3) _____ and admires, which is why he won.

B: He's also very brave and a great role (4) _____ for young people.

A: Yes, he certainly seems to have every (5) _____ that you could hope for in a policeman.

1. a. emergency   **b. community**   c. group   d. company
2. **a. hard-working**   b. outgoing   c. selfish   d. fierce
3. a. risks   b. achieves   **c. trusts**   d. stands out
4. a. human   b. man   c. person   **d. model**
5. **a. quality**   b. sense   c. behaviour   d. skill

C. Read the text below and complete the sentences giving examples which support the writer's opinion.

The person I admire more than anyone in the world is my mother. She is a nurse and she has saved many lives.

My mother is the kindest person I know. She is completely unselfish. **(1)** _She always helps others, no matter how tired she is_. She has spent all her life taking care of people. Few people are as reliable as my mother. **(2)** _She always does what she says she will._

My mother sometimes works at night and in the emergency room, so she deals with really stressful situations. She is also extremely patient. **(3)** _She has never complained about it, and she handles stressful situations well._

My mother has been a huge influence on me. **(4)** _Since I was a kid she has told me about helping people._ Thanks to her, I've decided to become a nurse, too. I want to offer as much as she does to those in need.

Everyone in the community knows and respects her and she is very sociable. **(5)** _She always talks to everybody if they have a health problem_. I want to be like her when I grow up.

▶▶ Student's Book pp. 26-27

A. Choose a, b, c or d.

You may not be **(1)** _____ with the Harry Winston Heist in 2008, but it's one of the most famous robberies. Four men dressed **(2)** _____ women entered the famous jewellery shop in Paris carrying guns and shouting at the assistants and customers there to 'get down!' People **(3)** _____ in fear and lay on the floor, as the men started filling their bags with jewels worth about $108 million. Within a few minutes, they had left the shop and had got **(4)** _____. Some of the jewels have been found and French police have arrested 25 suspects, but they are still **(5)** _____ the crime.

1. a. critical   b. remarkable   c. familiar   d. reliable
2. a. as   b. on   c. for   d. to
3. a. pulled   b. glanced   c. gasped   d. paused
4. a. away   b. off   c. out   d. over
5. a. reminding   b. gathering   c. working   d. investigating

B. Complete the sentences with the correct form of the words in capitals.

1. The weather is very _____ today. Let's go for a walk. — PLEASE
2. Queen Victoria had 78 _____ to provide her with anything she wanted. — SERVE
3. There has never been a _____ in our neighbourhood. — BURGLAR
4. We've _____ the furniture in the living room. I think it's better like this. — ARRANGE
5. Steven was surprised by his wife's _____ when he told her the news. — REACT
6. Ronnie Biggs is an English _____, best known for the Great Train Robbery of 1963. — CRIME

C. Complete the dialogue with the Past Simple or the Past Progressive of the words in brackets.

Olivia Hey, Jane. Where (1) _____ (be) you yesterday?
Jane I (2) _____ (not feel) well in the morning so I (3) _____ (stay) at home.
Olivia (4) _____ you _____ (hear) about the fire?
Jane Fire? What fire?
Olivia We (5) _____ (have) our Maths lesson when suddenly the fire alarm (6) _____ (go) off.
Jane Really?
Olivia Yeah. Mr Morris (7) _____ (tell) us all to leave the classroom and wait outside.
Jane Then what?
Olivia Well, as we (8) _____ (wait) in the playground, I (9) _____ (see) smoke coming from the 3rd floor. Luckily, there was nobody up there.
Jane What happened then?
Olivia The fire brigade (10) _____ (arrive) very quickly and put out the fire.
Jane Wow, I (11) _____ (hear) a fire engine yesterday morning as I (12) _____ (lie) in bed.
Olivia (13) _____ it _____ (go) down Maple Road?
Jane Yes.
Olivia Well, that was it then.

D. Complete the second sentence so that it has a similar meaning to the first sentence, using the word given. Do not change the word given. You must use between two and five words including the word given.

1. He heard a strange voice while he was walking into the house. **when**

   He was walking into the house _____ a strange voice.

2. After taking the train, we took the bus and went to the hotel. **then**

   We _____ we took the bus and went to the hotel.

3. The children were playing football when it started to rain. **while**

   It started to rain _____ football.

4. The phone rang and I woke up. **when**

   I _____ rang.

5. We were having a picnic when a dog ran over to us and stole a sandwich. **as**

   A dog ran over to us and stole a sandwich _____ a picnic.

6. I was walking down the street when I found a gold earring. **while**

   I found a gold earring _____ down the street.

▶▶ Student's Book pp. 28-29

A. Compete the sentences to form expressions with *keep*.

1. Keep _____ so I can cut your hair. Otherwise it won't be straight.
2. If Alice said she'll take you to the cinema, she will. She always keeps _____.
3. Slow down! We can't keep _____ you.
4. Keep _____ on the cake so it won't get burnt.
5. Please keep _____ the floor. It's wet and you may slip.
6. Can you keep me _____ while I wait for my taxi to arrive?

2b

B. Complete the sentences with the correct form of the words in capitals.

1. Unfortunately, the case is still under _____. **INVESTIGATE**
2. After the crash, he lay _____ waiting for help to arrive. **HELP**
3. I find it _____ that my brother found such an interesting job so quickly. **BELIEVE**
4. A loud _____ woke us up last night. **EXPLODE**

C. Choose a, b, c or d.

Weird plane accident!

Are you afraid of flying and hope that nothing will go wrong every time you have to fly? If the answer is no, you may find the following story quite amusing.

On 17 February 1994, the pilot of a Piper PA-34 fell asleep while he (1) _____ from Springfield, Kentucky to Crossville, Tennessee. He woke up five hours later and found himself over the Gulf of Mexico with 20 minutes of fuel left. It was a real (2) _____! The Cost Guard along (3) _____ an Air Force aircraft tried to help. They told him to go to the nearest airport (4) _____ was in Pinellas County, Florida. However, the plane didn't manage to reach the airport. It crashed into the ground as he was (5) _____ the airport. Fortunately, there were (6) _____ passengers on the plane and a Coast Guard helicopter quickly (7) _____ the pilot.

Anyway, accidents can always happen. (8) _____ people are afraid of travelling by plane. But you should keep (9) _____ mind that planes are one of the safest means of transport!

1. a. flew	b. was flying	c. fly	d. flying
2. a. panic	b. pause	c. scene	d. shock
3. a. of	b. with	c. to	d. and
4. a. where	b. who	c. which	d. whose
5. a. arriving	b. getting	c. going	d. approaching
6. a. not much	b. any	c. no	d. little
7. a. trapped	b. rescued	c. looked into	d. reacted
8. a. Lots	b. A lot	c. Much	d. Many
9. a. in	b. on	c. to	d. up

▶▶ Student's Book pp. 30-31

A. Match the words with their definitions.

1. therefore   a. the people that live in a particular place
2. search   b. speak very quietly
3. barely   c. take sth/sb from a place
4. whisper   d. as a result
5. locals   e. look for
6. remove   f. hardly

B. Complete the sentences with the words in the box. There are two extra words which you do not need to use.

| hope | surprise | real | eyes | minutes | breath | luck | true |

1. As I was fishing with my dad I saw a shark. It was a _____ shock!
2. The race was so exciting that we held our _____ until it was over.
3. A holiday in Paris sounded too good to be _____!
4. After driving around for hours we were sure that we were lost. There was no _____ left.
5. I couldn't believe my _____ when I saw a wolf outside our cabin!
6. We were out of _____. We couldn't find our map anywhere.

C. Complete the dialogue with the words/phrases in the box.

| in the meantime | as soon as | before | at first | the next thing she knew |
| because | as a matter of fact | while | so |

Mandy Where were you yesterday?

Lisa We went to Anna's house to surprise her (1) _____ it was her birthday.

Mandy Great! How did you surprise her?

Lisa Well, her mum sent her to the supermarket with a long list of things to buy. (2) _____ she left the house, we went in and started preparing everything. Erin and I were decorating the house (3) _____ her mum was making some snacks. (4) _____, her dad went to pick up the cake.

Mandy Really? Did you manage to finish everything on time?

Lisa Yes, of course. We were very well-organised (5) _____ everything was ready (6) _____ she returned.

Mandy Wow, great timing.

Lisa Yeah. (7) _____, just as I had finished decorating and everyone had arrived, her dad whispered to us that she was outside the house and that we should turn off the lights and stay quiet.

Mandy And then what happened?

Lisa Anna walked in and (8) _____, we shouted 'surprise!' (9) _____ she was so shocked that she couldn't speak, but then she saw it was us and was relieved and happy.

Mandy Wow, it sounds like a great birthday for her.

D. Read the following story. Rewrite it using the words given.

Last Friday a really funny thing happened during a Maths lesson at school. My Maths teacher Mr Hopkins was writing on the board.

It was so hot that I thought I was going to faint.	**so**
I asked to open a window.	
The windows were high up.	**for this reason**
Mr Hopkins helped me.	
I felt better.	**because**
The room was cooler and more comfortable.	
An enormous black bird flew in through the window.	**at that moment**
We saw the bird and we started laughing.	**as soon as**
We saw Mr Hopkins running around trying to catch the bird.	
We laughed even more.	**when**
The bird became tired.	**after a while**
It stopped on the bookcase.	**so**
Mr Hopkins climbed onto a chair and used his coat to catch the bird.	**immediately**
He carefully carried it to the window and set it free.	**finally**

It flew away and Mr Hopkins went back to the board. After such excitement, we found it hard to think about Maths. Our minds were still flying around in circles!

2 Round-up

A. Complete the text with the correct form of the words in capitals.

Are you looking for an (1) _____ book to read? Try one of Mark Twain's novels. Mark Twain was an American writer famous for his adventure stories and his (2) _____ collection of travel experiences. His two most well-known novels are *The Adventures of Tom Sawyer* (1876) and *The Adventures of Huckleberry Finn* (1884). Mark Twain did various jobs and gained a lot of (3) _____ experiences from them. For instance, while he was working as a steamboat pilot on the Mississippi River, he met many different kinds of people and heard several (4) _____ stories that he later used for his writings. Therefore, some of his stories were true while others were based on his (5) _____. Mark Twain was one of the most (6) _____ writers of his generation. This is why his work is (7) _____ and is still read today.

ENJOY
FORGET
USUAL
BELIEVE
IMAGINE
PASSION
REMARK

B. Choose a, b, c or d.

1. The pickpocket _____ away. The police couldn't catch him.
   a. got   b. went
   c. made   d. did

2. When Paula saw her son on TV, she _____ in surprise.
   a. leaned   b. glanced
   c. gasped   d. gained

3. She's got excellent communication skills and she can _____ with difficult customers, too.
   a. succeed   b. support
   c. manage   d. deal

4. Our trip to Prague was a _____. We didn't enjoy it at all.
   a. challenge   b. disaster
   c. harm   d. danger

5. He doesn't want to work under all this _____ any more. He needs some rest.
   a. panic   b. pressure
   c. shock   d. trouble

6. The teacher _____ at them as she was very annoyed with their behaviour.
   a. paused   b. dared
   c. landed   d. frowned

7. You can always _____ on me. That's what friends are for!
   a. rely   b. keep
   c. hold   d. set

8. The air conditioner is out of _____ again.
   a. work   b. use
   c. order   d. shape

C. Choose a, b, c or d.

1. That's the paramedic _____ I was telling you about.
   a. which   b. whose
   c. where   d. who

2. There _____ housework left to be done. Just the washing-up.
   a. isn't a   b. isn't much
   c. isn't any d. aren't many

3. _____ the smoke, he ran into the room.
   a. As soon as he saw   b. When he was seeing
   c. As he saw   d. While he was seeing

4. _____ in the street when a motorbike hit him.
   a. The boy was playing   b. While the boy was playing
   c. The boy played   d. As the boy played

5. _____ famous artists take part in this event every year.
   a. There are a few   b. Very little
   c. There are many   d. Very few

6. Johnny Depp, _____ acting I admire very much, stars in the film *The Tourist*.
   a. that the   b. who's
   c. whose   d. which

7. That's the cabin _____ we were staying.
   a. who   b. which
   c. whose   d. where

8. I heard noise outside and looked to see what _____.
   a. happen   b. was happening
   c. is happening d. happened

D. Read the magazine article about young people who do extreme sports. For questions 1-10, choose from the people (A-D). The people may be chosen more than once.

Which person says:

1. they do this sport with an expert?
2. they move fast over water when doing their sport?
3. they enjoy doing their chosen activity with friends?
4. they found they weren't very fit at first?
5. they only do this sport in pairs?
6. a lot of people wrongly think this sport is frightening?
7. they can end up in the air doing this sport?
8. they enjoy moving fast from high points doing this activity?
9. they go to various places to do this sport?
10. you have to look out for other people when doing this sport?

A

I have recently become very passionate about rock climbing. I find it really thrilling. At first it was very difficult as I wasn't in shape, and I wasn't strong enough to climb very high. I started going to the gym three times a week, and now I have no problem climbing for hours! It's a wonderful feeling climbing high above the ground and looking at the view. Sometimes I climb so high that I feel as if I can touch the sky! I'm not afraid any more and stay out of danger by following all the safety rules and by going with a climbing instructor.

B

Last summer I went on a camping holiday to the south of France and I tried kite-surfing. It was amazing! I already knew how to fly kites as my dad taught me when I was young, but using a kite on water was a whole new experience. If the wind is strong, the kite pulls you along extremely fast. It's unbelievable! You have to be careful of course and keep your eye on the water, in case of any rocks or other kite-surfers. By the end of the holiday, I had learnt how to do tricks and really high jumps. It was such a thrill!

C

I have been scuba-diving every summer for three years now and it is the best sport I have ever tried. The feeling of being underwater with so many fish and such incredible wildlife is fantastic. Some people think it's scary to be so deep underwater, but I just feel peaceful and happy down there. I haven't had any frightening experiences and I wouldn't say that I'm an especially courageous person. I had to complete a training programme in order to receive the certificate that allows me to dive. I always dive with a partner, which is the best way to stay safe. Anyone who loves the water should definitely try this sport!

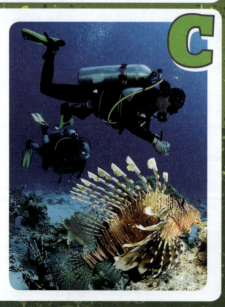

D

I fell in love with bicycles the moment I was old enough to learn how to ride on my own. Since that young age, I have had a variety of bicycles and my latest passion is mountain biking. I go every weekend with my friends to different places where it is exciting to ride. We usually try to go up some steep hills so that we can enjoy the feeling of quickly riding down again. We don't ride on roads, we go through forests and parks instead. We always get covered in mud but we don't care because we're having so much fun.

3a

▶▶ **Student's Book pp. 34-35**

A. Complete the text with the words in the box. There are two extra words which you do not need to use.

| off | buy | online | order | instructed | refund | discount | recommended | delivery | suitable |

my BLOG

Hi all,

I'd like to share my worst **(1)** _____ shopping experience with you. A friend **(2)** _____ a site where you can buy various gadgets at great prices. I went on the site and saw an MP4 player that I really liked and it had 15% **(3)** _____. Also, if I ordered within 24 hours, I would get an additional 10% **(4)** _____. It seemed like a great **(5)** _____ so I ordered it! Unfortunately, my enthusiasm didn't last for long.

The site said that **(6)** _____ would take 5 days, but I waited for my **(7)** _____ for 25 days! When the MP4 player finally arrived, I was shocked. The touchscreen didn't work! Can you believe it? The final straw was when I realised, a month later, that I had been charged the full price. I'm still waiting for a(n) **(8)** _____. I don't think I'll ever shop online again.

B. Match the words with their definitions. Then use some of the words to complete the sentences 1-5. Make any necessary changes.

1. technique   a. looking at items in shop windows without planning on buying them
2. shopaholic   b. the written information that tells you how to do or use sth
3. instructions   c. buying things believing that it will make you feel better
4. occasional   d. very impressive
5. shopping therapy e. someone who is addicted to shopping
6. spectacular   f. a short sleep, usually during the day
7. window-shopping   g. happening sometimes but not often
8. nap   h. a particular way of doing something

1. My sister is a(n) _____. Just look at her wardrobe. It's filled with clothes!
2. The _____ say that you have to assemble these parts first.
3. I think I'll take a(n) _____ after lunch because I've really tired myself out today.
4. Look at that _____ design on the ceiling.
5. **A:** Let's go on a shopping spree!

   B: No way. I haven't got any money. Let's just go _____.

3a

C. Choose a, b, c or d.

1. Those jeans don't fit her any more. She _____ lose some weight.
   a. needs to
   b. needs
   c. have to
   d. has

2. Bob doesn't _____ wake up early to go to school tomorrow. It's a holiday.
   a. has to
   b. must
   c. have to
   d. need

3. We _____ be late, because we will miss our flight.
   a. don't have to
   b. don't need to
   c. needn't
   d. mustn't

4. I'm afraid that you _____ leave your bicycle here.
   a. might not
   b. needn't
   c. don't need to
   d. can't

5. Mike _____ be home by now. His plane landed four hours ago.
   a. must
   b. can't
   c. can
   d. mustn't

6. Henry _____ come over today. He may finish work late.
   a. couldn't
   b. didn't need to
   c. might not
   d. can't

7. I _____ come to the concert tonight, but I'll give you a call later and tell you for sure.
   a. may
   b. can
   c. must
   d. could

8. Ann _____ be in her office right now. All the lights are off.
   a. mustn't
   b. can't
   c. needn't
   d. doesn't have to

D. Complete the second sentence so that it has a similar meaning to the first sentence, using the word given. Do not change the word given. You must use between two and five words including the word given.

1. It's possible that Helen won't invite them to her sleepover. **may**
   Helen _____ them to her sleepover.

2. It is certain that Michael isn't at the library. I just saw him at the park. **can't**
   Michael _____ at the library because I just saw him at the park.

3. Gary uses his father's car, so it isn't necessary for him to buy a car. **needn't**
   Gary uses his father's car, so _____ a car.

4. You are not allowed to eat in theatres. **mustn't**
   You _____ in theatres.

5. It isn't necessary for Kathy to do the washing-up. **have**
   Kathy _____ the washing-up.

▶▶ Student's Book pp. 36-37

A. Choose a, b, c or d.

A: Hey sis! Check this (1) _____! Isn't it cool?

B: Yes, it is. But Jenny, you bought so many clothes last month.

A: I know but look. They're on special (2) _____. You get two dresses (3) _____ the price of one.

B: Who cares? You'd better stop spending all your money on clothes.

A: Oh come on, you're making a big deal out of it. Anyway, I need a new dress for Mary's wedding.

B: OK fine. How much is it? Where's the price (4) _____?

A: It will probably cost you a(n) (5) _____ and a leg!

B: You're right. It's 150 euros.

1. a. out	b. off	c. up	d. in
2. a. sale	b. offer	c. discount	d. bargain
3. a. at	b. from	c. in	d. for
4. a. charge	b. coin	c. tag	d. note
5. a. hand	b. arm	c. foot	d. finger

B. Choose a, b or c.

1. Look, this jacket is half-price. It's a real _____!
   a. sale   b. value   c. bargain
2. I don't think we can _____ a trip to Europe this year.
   a. afford   b. cost   c. exchange
3. I'm totally _____. I can't go shopping with you.
   a. broke   b. short   c. bargain
4. This cool T-shirt came free of _____ with the magazine I've just bought.
   a. money   b. cost   c. charge
5. Don't worry, you can _____ euros into pounds at the airport.
   a. afford   b. bargain   c. exchange
6. A: Excuse me. You forgot your _____.
   B: Thank you very much.
   a. change   b. charge   c. exchange
7. Mary gets _____ on all the clothes in the shop where she works as a shop assistant.
   a. offers   b. discounts   c. sales
8. This offer is good _____ for money.
   a. value   b. price   c. worth
9. A: Would you like some help?
   B: No. I'm just _____.
   a. watching   b. seeing   c. browsing
10. Tomorrow is a bank _____. Shops are closed.
    a. day   b. holiday   c. celebration

C. Read the dialogues and circle the correct words.

1. A: What's wrong? You don't look very well.
   B: I think I have the flu.
   A: Then you **would rather not / had better not** go to school today.
2. A: Shall we go out tonight?
   B: **I'd rather / ought to** watch a DVD at home and order some pizza.
3. A: You **would rather / ought to** treat your sister better.
   B: Yeah, I guess you're right.
4. A: We're going to a rock concert tonight. Are you coming with us?
   B: Sounds fun... but I **would / wouldn't** rather not come. I need to study for my exam.
5. A: The shop isn't open 24/7, you know. You **would rather / had better** go before it closes.
   B: OK. I'll go in a few minutes.

D. Complete the second sentence so that it has a similar meaning to the first sentence, using the word given. Do not change the word given. You must use between two and five words including the word given.

1. I advise you not to speak to me like that again!   **had**

   You _____ to me like that again!

2. It's a good idea to look for offers when you go shopping.   **should**

   You _____ when you go shopping.

3. Len doesn't want to hang out at the shopping centre today.   **rather**

   Len _____ at the shopping centre today.

4. It's dangerous to drive fast in the rain.   **should**

   You _____ in the rain.

5. It's a good idea to tell your parents the truth.   **ought**

   You _____ the truth.

Student's Book pp. 38-39

A. Match. Then use some of the phrases to complete the sentences. Make any necessary changes.

1. open-air
2. mailing
3. mail order
4. department
5. shopping

a. address
b. market
c. catalogue
d. mall
e. store

1. This _____ has got over forty shops in it.
2. I'm looking through some _____. Come here and look at the shirt on this page. It's beautiful.
3. What's the _____? I don't know where to send the box.
4. It was raining, so we got wet while waiting for our sandwiches at the _____.

B. Complete the sentences with the correct form of the words in capitals.

Being a street vendor is a very interesting (1) _____ for three main reasons; you work outdoors, you meet lots of people and you're your own boss. If you want to become a street vendor, you should learn about and follow the procedures required to start your business. Then you should choose the product you want to sell. It's always a good idea to sell something people really need, such as food or something (2) _____, like accessories. What is also very important is the (3) _____. If the street market near your home is (4) _____ for you, don't worry. There are usually many places in the city where you can work, so do some research before selecting your spot. Of course, the best solution is to find other street vendors and ask for advice. And remember, you need to make sure that your (5) _____ is good because if your customers are happy, they will come again!

OCCUPY
FASHION
LOCATE
CONVENIENT
SERVE

C. Read the form Tanya has filled in. What has she done wrong? Find and correct her mistakes.

teen films homepage Join teenfilms.com to share your opinion about films and find reviews.

Complete the form below to get started (Fields with * are required)

First name*	Fisher	Postcode	0044 6903512267
Surname*	Tanya	e-mail address*	12 Hauser Street
Sex	✓ male ☐ female	Phone Number	M1 1AA
Mailing Address	tfisher16@hotmail.com		

D. Read the rest of the questionnaire and answer the questions.

1. What kind of films do you like?
   comedies ☐ adventure films ☐ horror films ☐
   science-fiction films ☐ animated films ☐
   romantic films ☐ other _____
2. How often do you watch a film?
   daily ☐ weekly ☐ monthly ☐ other _____
3. Where do you usually watch films?
   at home ☐ at a friend's house ☐ at the cinema ☐
   other ☐

4. Who do you usually watch films with?
   parent ☐ brother/sister ☐ friend ☐
   other _____
5. Would you like us to inform you about our new films by e-mail?
   yes ☐ no ☐

▶▶ Student's Book pp. 40-41

A. Complete the text with the words in the box. There are two extra words which you do not need to use.

rows   escalators   major   attracted   levels   maximum   displayed

AN ANCIENT SHOPPING CENTRE

The Stoa of Attalos, which is in the Ancient Agora in Athens, Greece, was one of the oldest shopping centres. It was built by and named after King Attalos II of Pergamos around 150 BC. The Stoa became the (**1**) _____ commercial building or shopping centre in the Agora and was used for centuries. It was a large building, 116 metres long and had two (**2**) _____ connected by two staircases. It had (**3**) _____ of rooms that were used as shops. It had 42 shops in all. The Stoa (**4**) _____ many people and soon became a place where merchants sold their products. They (**5**) _____ their goods and the Athenians gathered not only to shop but also to meet with other people and socialise.

B. Complete with the correct prepositions.

1. I'm sorry; I pressed the button _____ accident.
2. My younger brother thinks that he can get _____ with anything.
3. The travel agent helped us make the most _____ our trip.
4. We put _____ the meeting for two hours because nobody was ready.
5. Mark is likely _____ forget. He's got a horrible memory.
6. Unfortunately, Tom's company went out _____ business.

C. Circle the correct words.

1. **A:** You look tired.
   B: I **have been writing / have written** for two hours.
   A: Have you finished / Have you been finishing your short story yet?
   B: Not really. I can't think of a nice ending.
   A: Why don't you ask Jenny? She **has helped / has been helping** me many times with my homework.

2. **A:** Wow. Mary speaks Spanish fluently.
   B: I know. She **has studied / has been studying** Spanish for the past three years.
   A: That's good.
   B: Yeah and her brother **has moved / has been moving** to Spain.
   A: Really? **Has she visited / Has she been visiting** him?
   B: No. She **hasn't had / hasn't been having** any time. She's very busy with school.

3. **A:** Tina. What **have you done / have you been doing** all day?
   B: I **have tidied / have been tidying** my room.
   A: What about the rest of your chores?
   B: I **haven't done / haven't been doing** them yet.
   A: Remember, Tina. You promised.
   B: I know, Mum.

3b

D. Complete the text with the Past Simple, the Present Perfect Simple or the Present Perfect Progressive of the verbs in brackets.

I (1) _____ (not know) Carla for very long, but she is my best friend. We (2) _____ (meet) two years ago at the local youth club. We immediately (3) _____ (become) friends when we (4) _____ (discover) that we had the same interests. For example, both of us (5) _____ (collect) coins since we were five years old and have got big collections. We also like sports and (6) _____ (join) the local volleyball team. We (7) _____ (not play) in an important match yet, but we want to play in the next one, so for three months now we (8) _____ (train) very hard.

⏭ Student's Book pp. 42-43

A. Complete the sentences with the correct prepositions.

1. They managed to put _____ the fire before anyone was injured.

2. I don't understand how you could get _____ on so little money. You must be very good at managing money.

3. Peter put going to the dentist _____ till next week.

4. Many areas were affected _____ the storm.

5. I'm going to put my sister _____ until she finds her own flat.

6. Vivian never got _____ the shock of the shark attack.

B. Match. Then use the collocations to complete the sentences.

1. spare — a. skills
2. job — b. licence
3. motorbike — c. satisfaction
4. minimum — d. wage
5. people — e. time

1. He is too young to get a _____ so he rides his bike to school.

2. When Rob first started working in the company, he was earning _____.

3. You need to improve your _____ to become a camp leader.

4. Many people find happiness in _____ rather than in earning a lot of money.

5. Diana likes to go for a walk on the beach in her _____.

C. Here are some sentences about Jerry's new flat. For each sentence, complete the second sentence so that it means the same as the first. Use no more than three words.

1. Jerry was saving money for many years.
   Jerry was putting money _____ for many years.
2. Jerry bought the flat three weeks ago.
   Jerry has had the flat _____.
3. Jerry hasn't found the time to paint the kitchen yet.
   Jerry hasn't got _____ painting the kitchen yet.
4. Jerry decorates the flat when he isn't working.
   Jerry decorates the flat in his _____.
5. Jerry has a friendly relationship with all of his neighbours.
   Jerry gets _____ all of his neighbours.
6. His next-door neighbour listens to loud music but Jerry accepts it without complaining.
   Jerry puts _____ his next-door neighbour's loud music.

▶▶ Student's Book pp. 44-45

A. Complete the sentences with the correct form of the words in capitals.

1. Our _____ expects us to be trustworthy. — **EMPLOY**
2. She didn't have much _____ of European history. — **KNOW**
3. Mr Myers talked to us about the _____ of being polite to customers. — **IMPORTANT**
4. We can make an appointment at your _____. — **CONVENIENT**
5. Previous work experience will definitely be taken into _____. — **CONSIDER**
6. There were thirty _____ for the position. — **APPLY**

B. Choose a, b, c or d.

1. Peter is _____ in French. He's half French actually.
   a. foreign   b. fluent   c. punctual   d. well
2. If you have a problem, please _____ me. Let me give you my mobile number.
   a. contact   b. apply   c. require   d. regard
3. The meeting was delayed again because of Harry. He is never _____.
   a. grateful   b. full-time   c. punctual   d. literate
4. Nowadays, all children are computer _____.
   a. literate   b. affected   c. fluent   d. willing

C. Read the sentences a-g below. Which part of the letter/e-mail of application are they suitable for?

a. Furthermore, I consider myself to be very hard-working.
b. I would be grateful if you would reply as soon as possible.
c. In addition, I worked part-time at *La Pennes* for two years.
d. I am writing with regard to your advertisement in the Weekly News on 29th April.
e. I look forward to hearing from you.
f. I believe I am suitable for this position because I have all the necessary qualifications.
g. I am interested in applying for the job of a waiter at your restaurant.

Opening paragraph	
Main part	
Closing paragraph	

3b

D. Read the advertisement and the letter of application below. Find five sentences/phrases in the letter which are inappropriate and rewrite them.

Employer A & P
Location London
Job Type Full-Time

Apply to
A & P, West Road 37
London CR2 6XH

Personal Assistant needed for A & P trading company.
Applicants must be computer literate and speak German and Italian fluently.
They must also have organisational and communication skills, be trustworthy and be able to work under pressure.
Experience required.

Hello,

I am interested in applying for the position of personal assistant as advertised on the website searchforwork.com.

I think you should hire me because I'm really good. I am able to use a computer well and I am fluent in German, Spanish and Italian. I am also willing to work long hours if necessary.

Furthermore, I worked as a personal assistant in a sales company for five years. My previous job has given me the opportunity to improve my people skills, as well as learn how to deal with difficult situations. In addition, I consider myself to be well-organised and reliable.

Give me a call if you've got any questions about my application. I am available for an interview at your convenience. Please, write back soon.

Yours,
Nora Anderson

---

1. _____
2. _____
3. _____
4. _____
5. _____

3 Round-up

A. Choose a, b, c or d.

Hi Phil,

How's it going? Remember that you said you had loads of old stuff, and didn't know what to do with it? Well, I **(1)** _____ a great idea. Why not take it to a car boot sale? My cousin and I **(2)** _____ to one last summer and we got rid of lots of things, and made some money, too. First of all, you **(3)** _____ to buy a local newspaper and see when the next one is. I **(4)** _____ you choose a day when the weather will be nice, because you'll be standing outside all day. It's also good to have a table to **(5)** _____ your things. You **(6)** _____ go on your own, really. It's better if two people go. Hey! I can take you there in my car. That way you **(7)** _____ borrow your dad's car. I've got a few things I've been meaning to throw away, but I haven't got **(8)** _____ to it. I might be able to sell them. What do you think? It **(9)** _____ be a good laugh. Also, we can **(10)** _____ the most of the car boot sale and search for some **(11)** _____ for ourselves. We can find a wide **(12)** _____ of things, but we must make sure we don't come home with more than we take there!

Let me know what you think,
Harry

1. a. just have   b. 've just had   c. just have had   d. 've just been having
2. a. have been   b. have been going   c. went   d. was going
3. a. had   b. might   c. need   d. must
4. a. realise   b. recommend   c. warn   d. promote
5. a. attract   b. delay   c. display   d. put aside
6. a. ought not   b. 'd rather not   c. 'd better   d. shouldn't
7. a. may not   b. don't have to   c. can't   d. mustn't
8. a. over   b. on   c. along   d. round
9. a. has to   b. must   c. needs   d. could
10. a. make   b. take   c. have   d. do
11. a. coupons   b. refunds   c. sales   d. bargains
12. a. location   b. variety   c. standard   d. addition

B. Complete the second sentence so that it has a similar meaning to the first sentence, using the word given. Do not change the word given. You must use between two and five words including the word given.

1. I don't feel like going to the shopping centre.
   I _____ to the shopping centre.   **rather**
2. Penny hasn't got enough money at the moment.
   Penny _____ at the moment.   **short**
3. I'm sure Nancy is younger than Susan.
   Susan _____ than Nancy.   **must**
4. You can stay at my house for as long as you need.
   I'll _____ for as long as you need.   **put**
5. Maybe Larry is still at his job interview.
   Larry _____ at his job interview.   **might**
6. I advise you to start studying for your exams.
   You _____ for your exams.   **better**
7. Andrew started cooking thirty minutes ago.
   Andrew _____ thirty minutes.   **been**
8. There was no reason for you to come early.
   You _____ early.   **didn't**
9. You should avoid using your credit card so often.
   You _____ your credit card so often.   **ought**
10. The last time I saw Mary was before she moved to Brazil.
    I _____ she moved to Brazil.   **since**

33

C. Read the text and write T for True or F for False.

LET'S start trading!

Do you avoid going out because you haven't got enough money? Has your computer stopped working but you can't afford to fix it? Is it difficult to find a job where you live? There is a way to get many of the things you need, without any money. It's not a dream, and it's not against the law or complicated. It's the Local Exchange Trading System (LETS).

Here's how it works: Individuals, and sometimes businesses, get together to create a trading group. Each person or business in the group provides a service or product. For example, you might offer to babysit, or fix bicycles, or help elderly people do chores. Other group members may fix computers, do gardening or they might own a restaurant. All the services are advertised, often on a website. Every time you perform a service, you receive credits. You can then use your credits to get a product or service from another member of the group - for example a computer repair or a meal at a restaurant. No money is exchanged.

What are the advantages of LETS? The main one is that it saves you money. If you can buy some things with LETS credits, then you can keep your cash! Kate Burden, 23, never had enough money but couldn't find a part-time job that she enjoyed. So she joined LETS in Bristol last year, teaching English to people who were from other countries. 'With my first credits, I went to a local hairdresser and got a haircut without giving any money! It felt great,' she says. Kate also enjoys using credits to get local goods. 'My favourite discovery is a lady who makes amazing homemade cakes.' She also recommends LETS because it's a great way to meet people in your neighbourhood.

However, the system does have some disadvantages. There's always someone who uses services but doesn't provide any. To avoid this problem, many groups put a limit on how many credits you can owe the system. Another problem is that some goods and services are easier to trade than others, so you might not find what you want through LETS and have to look for it in the ordinary market, which requires money. But, if you are a quick learner, you can always offer services that you have not tried before and use them as an opportunity to learn new skills and find new interests.

Interested? Then look for a Local Exchange Trading System near you. LETS began in the USA and Canada, but now there are groups all around the world. A quick browse on the Internet and you are sure to find a group near you. So get connected, start trading services and put some money aside!

1. Only businesses can trade within the LETS system.
2. Not every person in a LETS group has to provide a service.
3. No payment in cash is made for LETS services.
4. A hairdresser cut Kate Burden's hair free of charge through LETS.
5. Kate Burden enjoys the social side of LETS.
6. Some people in LETS groups use more services than they provide.
7. You can find anything you want with LETS.
8. The LETS system has now spread to the USA and Canada.

Student's Book pp. 48-49

A. Choose a, b, c or d.

TEEN INVENTIONS

There are many creative and intelligent teenagers who never miss (1) _____ on experimenting. Such teenagers often (2) _____ that they can achieve major things. In fact, some of the most (3) _____ inventions have been teen inventions. This is just one example.

Blaise Pascal invented the first mechanical calculator to help his father with his work. In 1642 (4) _____ Pascal was still a teenager, he started working on his invention which was completed three years later. It was capable (5) _____ doing calculations quickly and effectively. At the time it had several names, like *Arithmetic Machine*, *Pascal's Calculator*, as (6) _____ as *Pascaline*. As the years passed, it was improved and finally became the modern calculator we know today.

1. **a.** from **b.** in **c.** out **d.** over
2. **a.** prove **b.** focus **c.** pass **d.** interact
3. **a.** individual **b.** financial **c.** unused **d.** outstanding
4. **a.** although **b.** regarding **c.** unlikely **d.** furthermore
5. **a.** from **b.** to **c.** of **d.** at
6. **a.** also **b.** well **c.** too **d.** good

B. Complete the crossword.

1. Your brother or sister is also called your _____.
2. If you don't succeed in doing something, you _____.
3. The study of numbers and measurements is called _____.
4. An untrue story or belief is also called a _____.
5. When someone gives lessons to another person, they _____ them.
6. If something is probably not going to happen, we say it's _____.
7. Something that is against the law is _____.
8. If we find a mistake in a text and put it right, we _____ it.

4a

C. Choose a, b, c or d.

1. _____ me some milk from the supermarket, please?
   a. Are you going to buy   b. Are you buying
   c. Will you buy   d. Will you have bought

2. Lisa _____ doing her homework before her father gets home.
   a. will be finished   b. is finishing
   c. will have finished   d. finished

3. By the time Jessie and Maria get up, we _____.
   a. will have left   b. are going to leave
   c. are leaving   d. will leave

4. Don't worry about the bike. I _____ it.
   a. fix   b. will fix
   c. will have fixed   d. would fix

5. Michael _____ his grandparents in New York this summer. He's already booked the tickets.
   a. will have visited   b. won't visit
   c. visits   d. is going to visit

6. Natalie _____ by seven o'clock.
   a. arrive   b. will have arrived
   c. is going to arrive   d. is arriving

7. Look at the grey clouds! It _____ rain.
   a. is going to   b. is having
   c. will be   d. will have

8. I _____ a motorbike next month. I've saved up most of the money.
   a. buy   b. will have bought
   c. am going to buy   d. would buy

D. Complete with the correct future form of the verbs in brackets.

1. _____ you _____ (help) me find my sunglasses, please?
2. Mike says he _____ (become) a doctor when he grows up.
3. I promise I _____ (not take) your things without asking again.
4. Hopefully, Frank _____ (return) from his trip by Monday.
5. Iris is sure she _____ (not get) a good mark in the exam.
6. Wait, I _____ (give) you a lift to the train station.
7. We _____ (not clean) this mess by the time my family gets back.

▶▶ Student's Book pp. 50-51

A. Complete the text with the correct form of the words in capitals.

Last year, my school arranged a student exchange programme in Germany. It was a bit expensive and, at first, my parents were (1) _____ to pay for it, but I persuaded them to. I was really excited about travelling to a(n) (2) _____ place.   **WILLING**

FAMILIAR

I stayed with a girl called Claudia and her family in a small village in Bavaria. Their village was beautiful. Claudia was great fun but her little brother was a bit annoying and (3) _____ so I preferred it when it was just the two of us. Unfortunately, Claudia's father didn't speak any English so, when I first arrived, we were (4) _____ of any communication. But by the end of the two weeks I was there, my German had improved a lot and we had some proper conversations. Of course, body language also helped.   **MATURE**

CAPABLE

Claudia is moving to Berlin next year, so it is (5) _____ that I'll ever visit her village again, which is a shame.   **LIKELY**

B. Complete the sentences with the correct prepositions.

1. I'm worried _____ James. Why is he so late?
2. J.K.Rowling is famous _____ her Harry Potter novels.
3. Children are not usually aware _____ the dangers around them.
4. I'm a bit nervous _____ my Geography exam.
5. Who's responsible _____ the car accident?
6. Ms Smith is very popular _____ students.
7. Laura is capable _____ looking after herself.
8. Are you familiar _____ this computer program?

C. Match the two halves.

1. Andrew loves History. He never misses
2. Tom was anxious
3. Do yourself
4. We are sitting
5. Jenny's parents were very disappointed
6. Please, make
7. Everyone was ready
8. They are very proud
9. Our teacher showed us how to do
10. That explanation doesn't make
11. I'm sorry. I made
12. Be careful! You'll make

a. of their daughter.
b. sure that you are here on time.
c. the experiment properly.
d. a lesson.
e. about going sailing because he gets seasick.
f. a favour and go home and relax.
g. for the big match.
h. a fool of yourself.
i. with her.
j. for a History exam tomorrow.
k. sense.
l. a mistake. I'll correct it now.

D. Complete the sentences with *all, both, neither, none, either*.

1. We've got two coffee machines but _____ of them works properly. We need to buy a new one.
2. All of my friends have already made plans, so _____ of them can hang out with me.
3. A: Which pair of shoes would you choose?
   B: _____. They're _____ awful.
4. _____ Frank and I want to go out, but _____ of us has got money, so we're staying at home.
5. I don't know where Mark and Len are. I haven't spoken to _____ of them since yesterday.
6. Penny and Bill like sports. _____ of them play basketball in the school team.
7. A: Would you like tea or coffee?
   B: _____. I don't really mind.
8. Tracy has three older sisters and _____ of them are teachers, like their mother.

4a

E. Rewrite the sentences using *either....or, neither...nor* **or** *both...and.*

1. Maria did well in the exam. Patrick did well in the exam, too.
   _____

2. We can go to the cinema or we can go to the new Japanese restaurant.
   _____

3. Fay hasn't revised for the exam. Ken hasn't revised for the exam, either.
   _____

4. My sister hates Maths. She also hates Geography.
   _____

5. Olivia will complete her studies this year or next year.
   _____

6. I haven't read the book or seen the film.
   _____

▶▶ Student's Book pp. 52-53

A. Complete the sentences with the words in the box. There are two extra words which you do not need to use.

eco-friendly	electronic	appealing	effective	motivating	compulsory	costly	benefit

1. Some developments in technology are still too _____ so many people are unable to buy them.
2. When DVDs first came out, they were _____ to customers because they were much smaller and lighter than video cassettes and did not break as easily.
3. Helen is a great teacher. She keeps finding new ways of _____ her students to learn.
4. Using the Internet is a very _____ way of doing research for schoolwork as you can easily and quickly find information on any subject.
5. English and German were _____ at my school. All the students had to take the classes.
6. Recently there has been a big increase in the sales of _____ products as more and more people are aware of the need to protect the environment.

B. Rewrite the sentences using the words in bold.

1. I like football but I don't want to play in a team. **although**
   _____

2. First of all, these old buildings are part of our heritage. **begin**
   _____

3. Using a mobile can be costly. It can also be harmful. **moreover**
   _____

4. I think we should all help make our town safer. **view**
   _____

5. At university, students learn a variety of skills, such as organisational skills. **example**
   _____

6. In my opinion, e-books are more convenient than paper books. **personally**
   _____

C. Complete the blanks with one word only.

Social networking sites have got a positive influence on our lives. Do you agree?

Yes, absolutely. Social networking sites have changed our lives for the better. To start (1) _____, they have made communication with friends so much easier, faster and cheaper. We do not have to worry about the cost and can chat free of charge for hours. What is (2) _____, we can communicate in a new way, for (3) _____, by sharing links to music and videos as we chat. We feel much closer to friends who live far away as we can keep up with what is going on in their lives through the photos they upload. It is as if we are all together in one community and distance no longer keeps us apart. The way I (4) _____ it, my social life has got better since joining a social networking site and I have more friends than ever before!

No, I disagree. From my point of (5) _____, social networking sites have not improved our lives or brought us closer and I believe this for many reasons. (6) _____ of all, nowadays we spend so much of our time communicating through computers that we don't spend any time face-to-face with our friends. (7) _____ that, I think that we can never really get to know the friends we make online and we only make shallow friendships. On social networking, instead of having ten true friends, we have one thousand virtual friends. I think that these friendships can actually make us lonelier than before as we spend so much time alone at our computers. (8) _____, I find this very sad as I think human beings need contact with each other. It is part of our nature.

4b

▶▶ **Student's Book pp. 54-55**

A. Choose a, b, c or d.

1. Peter wants to become a _____ superstar.
   a. legend b. global c. rhythm d. guest
2. My mother grew _____ in Mexico City.
   a. up b. on c. in d. out
3. Mark _____ in a local song competition and came second.
   a. entertained b. protested c. competed d. mixed
4. Justin Bieber recorded his _____ album *My World 2.0* in 2010.
   a. debut b. period c. brief d. lyrics
5. The music business is very _____.
   a. appealing b. competitive c. completed d. compulsory
6. Angela has proved her talent _____ and over again.
   a. under b. across c. again d. over
7. He has won many awards. _____ actual fact, he's won more than twenty awards.
   a. For b. To c. In d. At

B. Complete the dialogue with the words in the box. There are two extra words which you do not need to use.

compete   rhythm   beat   encourages   nonsense   era   roots   section

A: Wow! These kids can dance really well. How did they learn to move like that?
B: They go to a school that (1) _____ students to learn to dance, so they started young.
A: I wish I could dance well. Unfortunately, I have no (2) _____ and look silly when I try!
B: That's (3) _____! I saw you dance once and you were great!
A: Thanks, but I certainly wouldn't be able to (4) _____ with these kids. They are much better than me!
B: Well, I am too old to even try that kind of dancing. In my (5) _____, things were very different.
A: Yes, in those days you danced with a partner, didn't you?
B: Yes, and the music had a much slower (6) _____.

C. Choose a, b, c or d.
1. You _____ more time to do the things you like, if you become more organised.
   a. has   b. would have   c. may have   d. had
2. If you continue to practise the guitar, you _____ very good.
   a. would become   b. will become   c. become   d. becomes
3. I would not go to that restaurant, if I _____ you.
   a. am   b. will be   c. would be   d. were
4. If Kate wasn't such a talented musician, she _____ so popular.
   a. wouldn't be b. won't be   c. wasn't   d. don't be
5. Unless Sally _____ her seat belt, I won't drive her to the cinema.
   a. wore   b. wears   c. may wear   d. will wear
6. Patrick _____ very glad, if he knew he had won the competition.
   a. will be   b. be   c. is   d. would be
7. What would you do if you _____ a tiger?
   a. will see   b. would see   c. saw   d. see
8. If Erin gets there before me, _____ her to wait.
   a. must ask   b. ask   c. will ask   d. could ask
9. If you need an extra guitar player for your band, just _____ me a call.
   a. will give   b. would give   c. give   d. gave
10. Wood _____ if there isn't any air.
    a. doesn't burn b. don't burn   c. wouldn't burn   d. couldn't burn

D. Complete the second sentence so that it means the same as the first. Use no more than three words.
1. I don't think you should stay at that hotel.
   If I were you, I _____ at that hotel.
2. The weather is great so I am going for a walk.
   If the weather _____ great, I wouldn't go for a walk.
3. Sometimes the temperature reaches -15ºC. Then the lake freezes.
   When _____ -15ºC, the lake freezes.
4. Barry wants to study harder so he becomes a better student.
   If Barry _____, he'll become a better student.
5. Monica should hurry if she wants to get to the concert on time.
   Unless _____, she won't get to the concert on time.
6. Babies are often hungry. Then they cry.
   When _____, they cry.

Student's Book pp. 56-57

A. Circle the correct words.

1. Spain is a very **normal / common** holiday destination for northern Europeans.
2. Skateboarding is a very **popular / famous** hobby among teenagers.
3. Sue is a very **lively / alive** person. She always has a lot of energy.
4. Some teenagers try too hard to fit **up / in**.
5. My mother and my sister have very **same / similar** voices. I sometimes don't know who's talking to me on the phone!
6. This magazine **includes / contains** a computer game.
7. My twin brothers love to dress **same / alike** so people can mix them up.
8. Don't yell at him. He didn't break the window **for / on** purpose.
9. You should **apologise / blame** for your rude behaviour.
10. Henry **admitted / resisted** that he had made a careless choice.

B. Complete the blanks with one word only.

Health Matters!!

It is well-known that (1) _____ you haven't got a healthy diet, you put on weight. But this hasn't stopped the rise in obesity among young people across the world. Experts are worried (2) _____ this growing problem and blame lifestyle changes (3) _____ it. The numbers are already very high and if nothing is done, they will (4) _____ seriously increased by the year 2020. Experts argue that teenagers do not exercise enough or have a balanced diet. Though parents are aware (5) _____ the disadvantages of junk food, they find it difficult to bring (6) _____ their children away from junk food, as it is cheap and available everywhere. In addition, young people spend too much time playing computer games or watching TV, so they do not get the exercise they need to make up (7) _____ the extra calories they are consuming. It is not easy to include exercise in our daily routines, when most of our free-time activities now take place in front of a screen. However, if we do not take action now, we (8) _____ pay for it later. So at least try to get outside more. You won't regret it!

Student's Book pp. 58-59

A. Complete the text with the correct form of the words in capitals.

For James, even the (1) _____ of studying was boring. He only enjoyed playing football with his friends. He found reading books tiring and time (2) _____. His mother tried everything she could think of to make him study. But even when he had exams, he didn't do any (3) _____. At the end of the school year, he failed every subject so his parents decided not to allow him to play football as (4) _____. James felt very unhappy about this and he came to the (5) _____ that he would have to change his behaviour. He started studying more in the evenings after school and the next time he had exams, he passed every single one! His parents were very happy and said he could play football whenever he wanted.

THINK
CONSUME

REVISE
PUNISH
CONCLUDE

B. Put the sentences in the correct order to form a paragraph.

Furthermore, they tend to do better in their schoolwork. ○

There are many advantages to having a school uniform. ○

This is because they spend less time thinking about fashion and more time thinking about their studies. ○

For instance, students do not compare their clothes to others' or feel bad if they are not able to afford the latest fashion. ○

First of all, it helps all students feel equal and more confident. ○

C. Complete the blanks 1-6 in the essay with the missing sentences a-f.

Sports Day

1 ○ They are very popular events for lots of young people. However, for others they are quite unpopular.

2 ○ It is a day when they can have fun doing their favourite sport, as well as watch others take part in different activities. This day gives students the opportunity to feel that school is not only about studying, but also about performing well in other fields with their friends. **3** ○

4 ○ This is because they find the whole event unpleasant and they do not enjoy the pressure of competition. **5** ○

6 ○ Whether the advantages are more than the disadvantages depends on how the school deals with the whole event. In my opinion, it should be considered an opportunity for students to cooperate with each other and not compete. Also, it should not be compulsory for all students to take part in the events.

a For many students, sports day is the best day of the whole school year.

b School sports competitions, also known as 'sports days', are part of school life for many students all over the world.

c For example, children who are not good at sport find it especially difficult and feel embarrassed when they have to participate in races in front of the whole school.

d For instance, they can enjoy taking part in races and perhaps winning a prize at the end.

e On the whole, there are both pros and cons to having a sports day.

f On the other hand, for other students it is a very stressful day and they do not look forward to it at all.

4 Round-up

A. Choose a, b, c or d.

1. You should be _____ of yourself for behaving like that!
   a. frustrated
   b. ashamed
   c. disappointed
   d. distracted

2. We have to write an essay about the _____ and cons of using a car.
   a. pros
   b. processes
   c. plans
   d. points

3. The idea of buying this house is very _____ . It's so nice!
   a. effective
   b. motivating
   c. appealing
   d. encouraging

4. There's no _____ in trying to persuade me. I'm not changing my mind.
   a. point
   b. reason
   c. fuss
   d. version

5. The boy _____ up on the sofa and started reading his favourite comic book.
   a. curled
   b. spread
   c. replaced
   d. remained

B. Choose a, b, c or d.

1. If I were you, I _____ ask Tom for some help.
   a. will
   b. may
   c. should
   d. would

2. We may visit Mary _____ no time left.
   a. unless there's
   b. if there's
   c. unless there isn't
   d. if there won't be

3. I lent my sister both dresses but she didn't wear _____ of them.
   a. neither
   b. either
   c. none
   d. any

4. Either you _____ Robert will have to tell them the news.
   a. nor
   b. or
   c. and
   d. neither

5. Will you _____ your project before Ms Smith arrives?
   a. be completed
   b. has completed
   c. have completed
   d. completed

C. Complete the blanks with one word only.

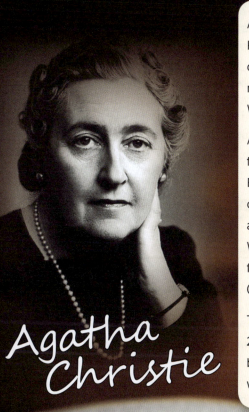

Agatha Christie was a famous writer of mystery novels, plays and short stories. People called her the "Queen of Crime" because she was capable (1) _____ writing crime novels that readers found difficult to put down. However, not (2) _____ her novels were crime novels; she also wrote romantic novels under the name Mary Westmacott.

Agatha was born and brought (3) _____ in Torquay, England. She travelled frequently and she used the knowledge and experiences she had in her novels. For Agatha, writing was probably a form (4) _____ expressing herself and getting over her shyness. She wrote more than 70 detective novels, as (5) _____ as an autobiography and several plays. Her first novel was *The Mysterious Affair at Styles*. What is more, she created two famous crime fiction characters, which you may be familiar (6) _____; Hercule Poirot and Miss Jane Marple. Many films about (7) _____ these characters have been made.

To sum (8) _____, Agatha Christie was one of the most creative writers of the 20th century. Over two billion copies of her books have been sold and her work has been translated into many languages. So, (9) _____ you like a good mystery, you will love Agatha Christie's novels!

D. Complete the blanks 1-7 with the sentences a-h below. There is one extra sentence which you do not need to use.

nature's CLASSROOM

When we hear the word 'school', most of us think of a class of students sitting in a room with a teacher by the board and books all around. **(1)** _____ However, for some, school is no longer closed inside four walls, but exists in open spaces with nature as the classroom. Over the past 50 years, there has been an increase in the number of schools opening that offer large parts of learning in outside spaces. The idea began in Sweden in the 1950s, but now they can be found across the United States and many other parts of the world. **(2)** _____

Supporters of outdoor learning argue that children benefit in many ways. Firstly, they can interact with the environment and learn about nature through touch, sound and smell as well as from the teacher. Secondly, it encourages children to be more active and so it helps them to stay healthy. What is more, children have fun while learning which is motivating and has been shown to have excellent results. **(3)** _____ This helps children learn to be responsible and caring members of the community.

(4) _____ It is based in the Kruger to Canyon Biosphere Region which is home to wild animals such as giraffes and elephants. Students at the school study the same subjects as other students in South Africa. However, in this school, the students also go out into the wild to learn. For example, young students practise Maths by counting the number of animals drinking from the water pools. **(5)** _____ This interactive learning has taught the students to respect wildlife and the environment and has also helped keep curriculum subjects lively and interesting.

Some people have argued that outdoor learning is expensive and also that it is difficult to control how children learn. **(6)** _____ Although it is true that these are real challenges for teachers, most people now agree that the benefits are more than the disadvantages and that children should be given the opportunity to experience at least some learning in nature's classroom. **(7)** _____

- **a.** One example of an outdoor school is in South Africa.
- **b.** This is what education has been like in many countries for the past few hundred years.
- **c.** They say it is hard to make sure they are doing what they are supposed to be doing.
- **d.** Older students measure the amount of water the animals drink and calculate how much water the animals will need over the next months.
- **e.** After all, seeing animals up close makes it easier to learn.
- **f.** Besides all this, it also involves activities that encourage teamwork, respect for others and the environment.
- **g.** Whatever your opinion of outdoor learning is, it is something that we are going to see more of in the coming years.
- **h.** But what makes them so special?

Student's Book pp. 62-63

A. Do the grid. Find: two water creatures, two bugs, two land animals.

B. Complete the sentences with the words in the box. There are two extra words which you do not need to use.

| set off | threat | announced | determined | attacked | facing | suffering |
| destruction | | strength | supplies | cross | isolated | |

1. They had to _____ the river so that they could reach the village.
2. I was walking in the forest when I was _____ by a bear.
3. More measures should be taken against the _____ of the rainforests.
4. He _____ for Madrid around three o'clock.
5. The manager of the company has _____ new measures.
6. You can find all kinds of office _____ in that shop.
7. Tanya has been _____ from backaches ever since the accident.
8. Peter has been _____ serious health problems lately.
9. He is unlikely to be a(n) _____ to our team. We will definitely win the final.
10. She is _____ to finish the project by the end of the week.

C. Choose a, b, c or d.

1. When James had finished his homework, he _____ to the skatepark.
   a. went   b. had gone   c. was going   d. had been going
2. By the time Fiona returned home, her daughter _____ the house.
   a. was tidied up   b. had tidied up   c. tidied up   d. had been tidying up
3. How long _____ for Kevin and his friend before they finally arrived?
   a. were waited   b. were waiting   c. had you been waiting   d. waited
4. After Ben _____ the documentary, he went to bed.
   a. was watched   b. was watching   c. had been watching   d. had watched
5. He realised that his school bag _____ still at home after he had reached the bowling alley.
   a. had been   b. been   c. was   d. was being
6. They _____ the restaurant by three o'clock.
   a. had been leaving   b. left   c. were leaving   d. had left
7. I had been ringing the bell for ten minutes before I _____ that I was at the wrong house.
   a. realised   b. was realising   c. had been realising   d. had realised

D. Complete the e-mail with the Past Simple, the Past Progressive, the Past Perfect Simple or the Past Perfect Progressive of the verbs in brackets.

Hi Linda,

What's up? You won't believe what **(1)** _____ (happen) to me yesterday. My cousins, Kate and Henry, **(2)** _____ (go) away for the weekend, so I **(3)** _____ (look after) their four-year-old daughter, Melissa.

Last night, after Melissa and I **(4)** _____ (play) games for four hours, we **(5)** _____ (decide) to go to bed. So, I **(6)** _____ (go) to the kitchen to get some milk for her, but when I **(7)** _____ (return) to the living room she **(8)** _____ (not be) there! I was so scared! As I **(9)** _____ (look) for her, I **(10)** _____ (notice) that Melissa **(11)** _____ (lie) under the sofa! She **(12)** _____ (sleep) there for a while before I **(13)** _____ (find) her. As it **(14)** _____ (turn out), she **(15)** _____ (hide) there as a joke but she **(16)** _____ (fall asleep) instead. I don't think I'll ever babysit again!

Take care,
Adrianna

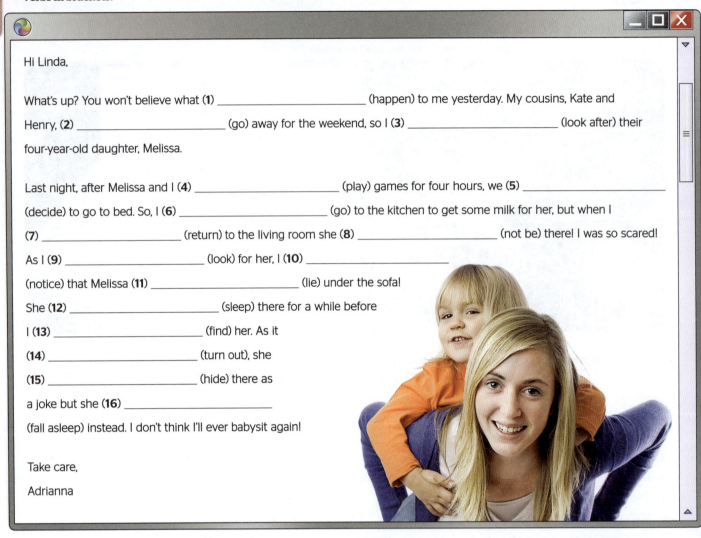

▶▶ Student's Book pp. 64-65

A. Choose a, b, c or d.

1. If we aren't at the airport in twenty minutes, we'll miss our _____.
   a. flight   b. cruise   c. voyage   d. journey
2. After driving for hours, they finally _____ at the village.
   a. got   b. arrived   c. approached   d. reached
3. My brother has decided to set _____ his own business.
   a. off   b. up   c. out   d. on
4. We're thinking of going on a(n) _____ down the Nile.
   a. cruise   b. flight   c. expedition   d. tour
5. Paul was chosen as the band _____ because he's the most talented.
   a. chief   b. boss   c. guide   d. leader
6. They won't _____ Paris until eight o'clock in the morning.
   a. get   b. arrive   c. reach   d. approach
7. We went on a guided _____ around the museum.
   a. trip   b. tour   c. excursion   d. expedition
8. Mark's _____ told him not to come to work late again.
   a. guide   b. chief   c. leader   d. boss

B. Complete the sentences with the correct form of the words in capitals.

1. The Alpine regions are perfect for _____ who wish to keep fit during their holidays. **TRAVEL**
2. _____ can enjoy wonderful tours through beautiful green valleys and mountain paths. **CYCLE**
3. Climbing ice walls isn't easy so you will definitely need an _____. **INSTRUCT**
4. In 2010 The Louvre in Paris had around 8.5 million _____. **VISIT**
5. The _____ at the hotel was very polite. **RECEPTION**
6. He works as a TV _____ in New York. **REPORT**
7. The ticket _____ asked to see our tickets. **INSPECT**
8. The Julian Alps in Slovenia is a very popular destination for _____. **SKI**

C. Rewrite the sentences using Reported Speech.

1. The doctor always says, 'You should wash your hands before eating.'
   _____

2. 'I will visit my cousin tomorrow,' said Gabriella.
   _____

3. 'I bought a beautiful pair of earrings last weekend,' said Aunt Helen.
   _____

4. Robert said, 'I'm flying to Chicago tonight.'
   _____

5. 'The boys are already asleep because they are waking up early tomorrow,' Karen told Stu.
   _____

6. 'Georgina can help you with the cooking,' Rita said to me.
   _____

7. 'You must be at the train station early in the morning,' Jack told us.
   _____

D. Rewrite the sentences using Reported Speech and the verbs given. Make any necessary changes.

1. 'I will book the tickets,' Tom said to his brother. — **promise**

2. My sister said to me, 'I can help you finish your homework.' — **offer**

3. 'I broke the window,' the student said to the teacher. — **admit**

4. 'I didn't lie to you,' Daniel said to his friend. — **deny**

5. 'OK, we can trek across the mountains of central China,' Alan said to Alice. — **agree**

6. 'I can't join you because I have a lot of work to do,' Penny said to us. — **explain**

7. 'Let's ask the man at reception,' said Sandra. — **suggest**

▶ Student's Book pp. 66-67

A. Complete the sentences with the correct form of the words in capitals.

1. After the long walk up the mountain, the trekkers felt _____. — **EXHAUST**
2. I forgot my gloves and my hands were _____. — **FREEZE**
3. James was _____ when his new computer arrived. — **DELIGHT**
4. The Prime Minister gave a _____ speech about the local youth club last week. — **FASCINATE**
5. The food at that restaurant was _____. I couldn't eat it. — **DREAD**
6. The Burden family had a _____ holiday in Cornwall last summer. — **MARVEL**
7. When Mrs Morris saw the mess the children had made, she was absolutely _____. — **FURY**
8. After playing football, Michael's shorts were completely _____. — **FILTH**
9. He was _____ by his exam results. He had not expected to do so well. — **ASTONISH**

B. Complete the sentences with the correct prepositions.

1. She nearly jumped _____ of her skin when she saw the spider on the bed.
2. When Tom was accepted into Oxford University, he was _____ the moon.
3. Jenny used to always play tricks _____ her younger brother.
4. When the fire alarm went off, everyone rushed _____ of the house.
5. My heart was _____ my mouth during the whole exam.
6. My younger brother drives me _____ the wall.
7. I felt _____ top of the world when I won the tennis match.
8. She's a real pain _____ the neck.

C. Read the account of a true event. Replace the highlighted words with a strong adjective.

It was the last day of my summer holiday in Spain. I was staying with my family in the south of Spain. It was a ① very nice location with lots to see, such as a ② very big castle and a ③ very interesting museum. Every morning before we started our busy day, I would get up early and go to the market to buy fresh fruit and vegetables. So, I became friends with the market traders who were pleased to see me and greeted me with friendly smiles.

So, on that day I had my camera with me and I asked some market traders to stand together for a photo. 'Of course!' they replied and they got ready for me to take the photo. I was looking through my camera and walking backwards when suddenly, I felt my legs slip. I fell to the ground and at the same time knocked a stall over. All the produce went flying into the air and fell on top of me. But it wasn't fruit. It was thousands of ④ very small fish and they were all over me. I was ⑤ very dirty.

I went red as a beetroot! Everyone in the market burst out laughing which made me feel ⑥ very angry. In the end, I saw the funny side of it and started laughing too. I gave the man at the fish stall my camera and he took a photo of me covered in fish. I laugh every time I look at that photo and now I don't think it was a ⑦ very bad experience after all.

1. _____ 2. _____ 3. _____ 4. _____
5. _____ 6. _____ 7. _____

Student's Book pp. 68-69

A. Choose a, b, c or d.

1. Heather wore very smart clothes to her job interview to make a good _____.
   a. impression   b. gesture   c. delight   d. outing

2. It is illegal to _____ litter on the side of the road. But unfortunately many people still do it.
   a. set   b. dump   c. rest   d. roam

3. The exam was a _____ of cake. Of course, I had studied very hard for it.
   a. piece   b. slice   c. part   d. bit

4. What time does the sun _____ during summer?
   a. sit   b. set   c. leave   d. go away

5. After spinning around in circles, the girls felt very _____.
   a. dizzy   b. magical   c. nervous   d. furious

6. It was such a(n) _____ to see my grandparents at the weekend.
   a. impression   b. delight   c. wonder   d. issue

7. Winning the competition was a dream come _____.
   a. alive   b. true   c. real   d. right

B. Match. Then use the phrases to complete the sentences.

1. give   a. a taxi
2. grab   b. his mind
3. live   c. up to his expectations
4. hail   d. a bite
5. cross   e. it a try

1. When Jack left the house, it started raining so he decided to _____.
2. He was working so hard all day that he missed lunch and had to _____ on the way home.
3. I know skateboarding looks difficult but you should _____. It's lots of fun.
4. Alex was really disappointed by the film. It didn't _____.
5. Peter searched the entire house for his car keys. But it did not _____ to check his pockets.

C. Rewrite the following sentences using Reported Speech.

1. 'What size are you?' the shop assistant asked me.

   The shop assistant wanted to know _____

2. 'Eat your kebabs, children!' said Mrs Stevens.

   Mrs Stevens told the children _____

3. 'Excuse me, do you know the way to the post office?' the woman said to me.

   The woman asked me _____

4. 'Don't talk with each other during the lesson!' the teacher said to her students.

   The teacher told her students _____

5. 'Take an umbrella with you when you go out' Fred said to Jill.

   Fred told Jill _____

6. 'Could you open the window, Robert?' said Mike.

   Mike asked Robert _____

D. Rewrite the sentences using the verbs given and Reported Speech. Make any necessary changes.

1. 'Stand behind the line,' said the security guard. **tell**
   _____

2. 'Why was John crying yesterday?' Henry asked. **wonder**
   _____

3. 'Jack, what time does the show begin?' said Eric. **ask**
   _____

4. 'Put your hands above your head!' the policeman said to the man. **order**
   _____

5. 'Where did you learn to speak Arabic so well?' Kathy asked Helen. **want to know**
   _____

6. 'Don't step on my puzzle!' Ben said to me. **tell**
   _____

▶▶ Student's Book pp. 70-71

A. Complete the text with the words in the box.

| landed | baggage | delay | boarding pass | fasten | departing | check in | took off | clerk |

Last summer, I went on my first trip by plane. Although I was all alone, I did pretty well. When I arrived at the airport, I immediately went to (1) _____. I gave my passport to the check-in (2) _____ and I asked for a window seat so I could see the view. Fortunately, there were some left. After that, he checked in my (3) _____ , gave me my (4) _____ and told me that my flight was (5) _____ in half an hour. However, there was a problem with the plane and there was a three-hour (6) _____! When I finally got on the plane, I was told to (7) _____ my seat belt. After a few minutes the plane (8) _____. I was very excited but also very exhausted. I fell asleep and woke up just when we (9) _____ at our destination. So much for the view!

5b

B. Match the words with the definitions. There are two extra words which you do not need to use.

| passport | on board | aisle seat | gate | flight attendant | airline | hand luggage |

1. _____: a place in an airport where passengers board their plane

2. _____: on a ship, plane or spacecraft

3. _____: a person whose job is to serve and take care of passengers on a plane

4. _____: an official document that you get from the government that proves who you are and allows you to travel abroad

5. _____: small bags that you take with you on the plane

C. Complete the text with the correct form of the words in capitals.

My grandparents are still very active and they have always loved to travel. Last summer, they decided to visit some friends in Sydney, Australia. They were looking for tickets online but couldn't find any good prices. Finally, a friend of a friend who worked in a travel agency found some (1) _____ tickets for them. On the day of their flight they were very excited. The shock came later, on the plane. After the pilot's (2) _____, they realised that they were actually flying to Sydney, Nova Scotia, in Canada instead of Australia.

EXPENSIVE

ANNOUNCE

Grandpa started laughing nervously but grandma got very upset. She couldn't believe that they hadn't paid any attention to the (3) _____ board at the airport or their (4) _____ passes.

DEPART

BOARD

Fortunately, the air crew were all very helpful and (5) _____ and tried to calm them down. They called us two hours after their (6) _____ in Canada to let us know what had happened. They had a very nice time there but I'm sure they'll never forget this experience.

FRIEND

ARRIVE

⏭ Student's Book pp. 72-73

A. Match. Then use some of the compound nouns to complete the sentences.

1. nature   a. site
2. archaeological b. crossing
3. ancient   c. spot
4. sign   d. sign
5. stop   e. ruins
6. pedestrian   f. post

1. She made her way across the road at a _____.
2. The driver who hit my car hadn't seen the _____.
3. One of the best _____ in the world is Yellowstone National Park in Western USA where you can find some amazing wildlife.
4. After thirty minutes of driving, we saw a _____ showing the direction and distance to the village.

B. Read the sentences a-h below and put them next to the correct heading in the box, depending on what they express.

a. How do I get from the station to the theatre?
b. What do you think about visiting the National Museum?
c. It's on the corner of Maple Street.
d. Can you tell me the way to the art gallery, please?
e. There is a Chinese restaurant nearby that you'll love.
f. Take the second turning on the left.
g. Go straight on for about 300m until you come to the cinema.
h. Something we shouldn't miss is the World Photography Festival.

Suggesting	
Asking for directions	
Giving directions	

C. Your cousin, who lives abroad, has decided to visit you. Look at the map and complete the letter to your cousin giving him/her directions to your house and suggesting some things you can do while he/she is in town.

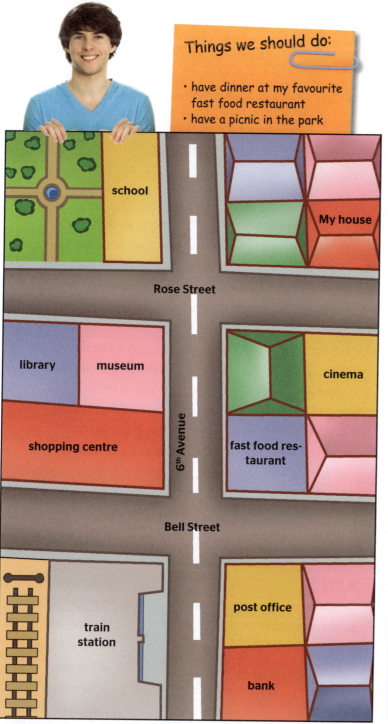

Things we should do:
• have dinner at my favourite fast food restaurant
• have a picnic in the park

Dear _____,

I'm so glad you are paying me a visit. We haven't seen each other for ages! There are lots of things to do here, so I'm sure we'll have a great time.

Unfortunately, I can't pick you up from the train station because I'll be babysitting Julie. You see, both Mum and Dad will be working on Saturday morning. But don't worry because getting to my house is pretty easy. The station where you get off is on _____
_____
_____
_____
_____
_____

I can't wait to see you. There are so many things we can do together. We should definitely _____
_____
_____
_____
_____
_____
_____

Anyway, I have to go now. So if you have any trouble, call me on my mobile. Have a safe trip!

Best wishes,
Andrew

5 Round-up

A. Complete the second sentence so that it has a similar meaning to the first sentence, using the word given. Do not change the word given. You must use between two and five words including the word given.

1. He felt great.
   He felt _____ the world.   **top**

2. He was very embarrassed.
   He wanted the ground _____ him.   **swallow**

3. 'Will you travel to Paris by train?' Lisa asked me.
   Lisa wondered _____ to Paris by train.   **whether**

4. Mark is very annoying sometimes.
   Mark is sometimes a _____ neck.   **pain**

5. 'Please don't turn on your mobile yet,' said the flight attendant.
   The flight attendant _____ turn on my mobile yet.   **asked**

6. She stopped at the café and got something to eat.
   She stopped and _____ at the café.   **grabbed**

7. 'You must try harder,' said my English teacher.
   My English teacher _____ try harder.   **told**

8. 'Do you know who swam in the swamp, Charles?' Dave asked.
   Dave asked Charles _____ swum in the swamp.   **if**

B. Read the text and choose a, b, c or d.

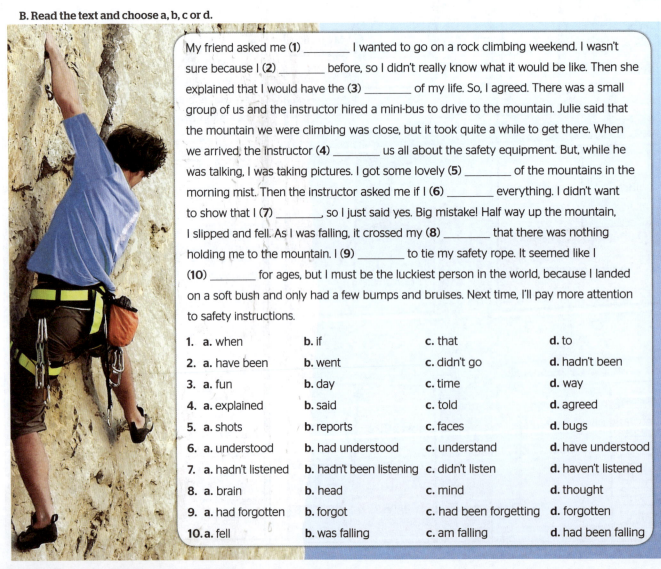

My friend asked me (1) _____ I wanted to go on a rock climbing weekend. I wasn't sure because I (2) _____ before, so I didn't really know what it would be like. Then she explained that I would have the (3) _____ of my life. So, I agreed. There was a small group of us and the instructor hired a mini-bus to drive to the mountain. Julie said that the mountain we were climbing was close, but it took quite a while to get there. When we arrived, the instructor (4) _____ us all about the safety equipment. But, while he was talking, I was taking pictures. I got some lovely (5) _____ of the mountains in the morning mist. Then the instructor asked me if I (6) _____ everything. I didn't want to show that I (7) _____, so I just said yes. Big mistake! Half way up the mountain, I slipped and fell. As I was falling, it crossed my (8) _____ that there was nothing holding me to the mountain. I (9) _____ to tie my safety rope. It seemed like I (10) _____ for ages, but I must be the luckiest person in the world, because I landed on a soft bush and only had a few bumps and bruises. Next time, I'll pay more attention to safety instructions.

1. a. when   b. if   c. that   d. to
2. a. have been   b. went   c. didn't go   d. hadn't been
3. a. fun   b. day   c. time   d. way
4. a. explained   b. said   c. told   d. agreed
5. a. shots   b. reports   c. faces   d. bugs
6. a. understood   b. had understood   c. understand   d. have understood
7. a. hadn't listened b. hadn't been listening c. didn't listen   d. haven't listened
8. a. brain   b. head   c. mind   d. thought
9. a. had forgotten b. forgot   c. had been forgetting d. forgotten
10. a. fell   b. was falling   c. am falling   d. had been falling

C. Read the text and choose a, b, c or d.

Ferdinand Magellan

Ferdinand Magellan was a famous Portuguese explorer who gave the Pacific Ocean its name. The name means that it is a calm and peaceful ocean. He also led the first expedition that sailed around the world from 1519 to 1522, although he himself did not finish the journey.

At first he sailed for his native country, Portugal. But when the Portuguese King Manuel II refused to let him lead an expedition to the Spice Islands in Indonesia, he decided to leave Portugal and go to Spain. The Spice Islands were very rich in spices which people could trade around Europe and which provide them with important financial benefits. At that time, Spain was in competition with Portugal for business and was looking for new routes to get to the Far East in order to trade. Portugal controlled the route that went around the South of Africa and then East towards India, so Spain needed to find a new route. Magellan planned an expedition that would reach the Spice Islands by crossing west over the Atlantic and then go around the southern part of Chile. He presented his plan to King Charles V of Spain, who immediately agreed to it. It was a great solution for Spain to continue trading without upsetting their neighbour, Portugal.

The voyage began in September 1519, and lasted until September 1522. Magellan sailed from Seville, Spain, with five ships, the *Trinidad*, *San Antonio*, *Concepción*, *Victoria* and *Santiago*. Three years later, only one ship (the *Victoria*) made it back to Seville, carrying only 18 of the original 270 crew members. Magellan was killed towards the end of the voyage, on the Island of Mactan in the Philippines, during a battle with the natives. The navigator Juan Sebastián Elcano completed the trip. It was the first expedition to sail across the Atlantic and into the Pacific Ocean. It was also the first to sail around the world, even though this had not been Magellan's plan. His goal was just to reach the Spice Islands and then to return the way he had arrived. However, after his death Elcano made the decision to continue the expedition Westwards around the south of Africa.

Even if it was not Magellan's plan to sail around the world, there is no doubt that he led one of the most important naval expeditions in history and will always be remembered as a great world explorer.

1. What was Magellan the first to do?
   a. Give a name to the Pacific Ocean.
   b. Sail around the world.
   c. Trade spices from the Far East.
   d. Sail for Portugal.

2. Why did Magellan leave Portugal for Spain?
   a. The Portuguese king told him to.
   b. The Spanish king invited him.
   c. The Portuguese king did not agree to his planned expedition.
   d. The Portuguese ships could not sail East to the Spice Islands.

3. What was Spain trying to find?
   a. A new business plan with Portugal.
   b. A new way to get to the Far East for trade.
   c. A way to sail to Chile.
   d. A way to build a larger ship.

4. Why did the King think the expedition was a good idea?
   a. It was a safe and easy journey.
   b. It would not cost a lot.
   c. It would avoid problems with Portugal.
   d. It would be an interesting exploration.

5. Magellan's expedition returned after 3 years with
   a. half the number of ships it had left with.
   b. five ships but with half the crew.
   c. only 18 men including Magellan.
   d. 18 men but without Magellan.

6a

▶▶ Student's Book pp. 76-77

A. Choose a, b, c or d.

1. It is important to wear _____ clothing to job interviews so as to make a good impression.
   a. basic   b. appropriate   c. urban   d. effective

2. The teacher told Sandra to be quiet but she carried _____ talking anyway.
   a. on   b. in   c. over   d. to

3. During the chess match, Patrick tried not to show his _____ that he was nervous.
   a. opponent   b. obstacle   c. attitude   d. response

4. The Tower of London is one of London's most famous _____.
   a. gaps   b. philosophies   c. landmarks   d. arts

5. It really winds me _____ when people use their mobile phones in the cinema.
   a. down   b. up   c. over   d. out

6. Flight 5206 to Paris has been _____ because of bad weather conditions.
   a. interrupted   b. beaten   c. cancelled   d. broadcast

7. Linda was so happy to arrive at the port that she _____ off the boat before it had even stopped moving.
   a. rolled   b. dived   c. overcame   d. lept

8. The location of the event depends _____ the city council's decision.
   a. to   b. on   c. for   d. with

9. Hearing my grandmother's voice on the phone really _____ my day.
   a. had   b. got   c. did   d. made

10. This channel has got too many _____.
    a. commercials   b. obstacles   c. gaps   d. landmarks

B. Complete the sentences using the Passive Voice.

1. The players must never interrupt their coach.

   The coach _____

2. Jasper's parkour tricks entertained us for hours.

   We _____

3. Emma will give him the instructions tomorrow.

   The instructions _____

4. People should always wear a helmet when riding a motorbike.

   A helmet _____

5. My mother has already bought all the necessary ingredients for the cake.

   All the necessary ingredients for the cake _____

6. The children broke the bottle while they were playing.

   The bottle _____

7. Every day they bring fresh fruit and vegetables to our restaurant.

   Fresh fruit and vegetables _____

C. Rewrite the following sentences using the Passive Voice. Write the sentences in two ways, as in the example.

1. Harry will give him some advice.

    He will be given some advice by Harry.

    Some advice will be given to him by Harry.

2. Jackie sent Helen a birthday card last week.

    _____

    _____

3. Peter will give me the money tomorrow.

    _____

    _____

4. The company has just offered Emma a job.

    _____

    _____

D. Complete the dialogue with the expressions in the box.

a. having a whale of a time
b. a bit of a downer
c. bored stiff
d. getting on my nerves
e. get a kick out of
f. thrilled to bits

Daniel This play is terrible! I'm (**1**) _____. Can we leave?

Alan But why? I'm (**2**) _____. These actors are so funny!

Daniel I can't stand it. The people in front of us keep laughing really loudly. It's (**3**) _____.

Alan Oh come on, it's a comedy! You're being (**4**) _____.

Daniel I'm sorry but I don't (**5**) _____ sitting in the theatre with all these noisy people. I'm leaving!

Alan OK OK... But let's leave quietly. The actors won't be (**6**) _____ if they see us leaving.

▶▶ Student's Book pp. 78-79

A. Complete the sentences with the correct prepositions.

1. Iris apologised _____ breaking my MP4 player.

2. His back injury prevented him _____ playing in today's game.

3. In 2003 scientists began a search _____ the Lost City of Atlantis off the south coast of Spain.

4. Sheila was afraid that she wouldn't be able to cope _____ so much work.

5. Be quiet! I can't concentrate _____ what I'm doing.

6. Young people in the city centre have been able to benefit _____ the new youth club that has been built.

7. It's important that children are given the opportunity to interact _____ other children their age.

8. I insist _____ driving you home.

6a

B. Complete the sentences with the correct form of the words in capitals.

1. A car is a _____ if you live in the countryside. **NECESSARY**
2. Mike has got a bit of a _____ problem. **WEIGH**
3. There has been a _____ in the number of students who become addicted to computer games. **GROW**
4. We need to raise _____ about the dangers of smoking. **AWARE**
5. Regular physical _____ will help you stay in shape. **ACTIVE**
6. I really need to improve my _____. **FIT**
7. Sally's chicken was _____ and dry. **COOKED**

C. Complete the sentences with the correct passive form of the verbs in brackets.

1. The bridge _____ (design) by a French architect in the 19th century.
2. A protest _____ (organise) for next week.
3. We were having a meeting while our meal _____ (prepare).
4. At the hotel, breakfast _____ (serve) every day between 8 and 10 o'clock.
5. The workers _____ (surprise) by the owner's decision to change the company's name.
6. What _____ (include) in the price?
7. The garden _____ (water) by the gardener right now.
8. Why _____ (the house / not clean) yet?

D. Complete the second sentence so that it means the same as the first. Use no more than three words.

1. People saw Kristie leave work early yesterday.

   Kristie was _____ work early yesterday.

2. Tony is putting the important documents in his office.

   All the important documents _____ in Tony's office.

3. In the past people believed that the Earth was flat.

   In the past the Earth _____ be flat.

4. People think that she is the most beautiful woman in the world.

   She is _____ the most beautiful woman in the world.

5. My father made me do my homework as soon as I got home.

   I _____ do my homework as soon as I got home.

6. People say that eating too much red meat is bad for our health.

   Eating too much red meat is _____ bad for our health.

7. Somebody heard the children calling for help.

   The children _____ calling for help.

Student's Book pp. 80-81

A. Complete the sentences with the correct form of the words in capitals.

1. Let me give you a _____ of how this camera works.   **DEMONSTRATE**
2. He's a wonderful _____.   **PERFORM**
3. Lunch and _____ are included in the price.   **REFRESH**
4. All _____ were asked to complete a questionnaire.   **PARTICIPATE**
5. Student _____ starts in the middle of September.   **REGISTER**

B. Complete the blanks with one word only.

VIDEO GAME WORKOUT

Research has proven that physical activity helps you control your weight and cope (**1**) _____ stress and health problems. It can also prevent you (**2**) _____ getting ill. Gyms usually offer various fitness programmes you can choose from. And if these programmes (**3**) _____ followed, then the benefits are obvious. However, if you don't want to sign (**4**) _____ at a gym because you find the whole idea a bit boring, there is another alternative: video gaming. Today there are many video games that require body movement, called exergames. Exergames (**5**) _____ first introduced in the early 2000s, but their roots can (**6**) _____ found in some games of the 1980s. In some ways they (**7**) _____ related to virtual reality because you interact in a similar way. However, the difference is that you have to move around a lot depending (**8**) _____ what you see on the screen. In the past, playing video games meant sitting on the sofa. With exergames you play sports, dance, do aerobics, martial arts and many other activities. But it's not all about exercise. As in most games, you need to concentrate (**9**) _____ what you are doing, so you exercise both your body and mind. With exergames, instead of being bored stiff at the gym, you can have a whale (**10**) _____ a time while exercising in the comfort of your home. (**11**) _____ doubt, you're thinking this is too good to be true. Well, it is but you should just be careful. Experts say you shouldn't overdo it! It's OK to spend a couple (**12**) _____ hours per week playing these games, but getting outside for some fresh air is also necessary for a healthy lifestyle.

C. Read the questions and complete the bubbles, forming indirect questions.

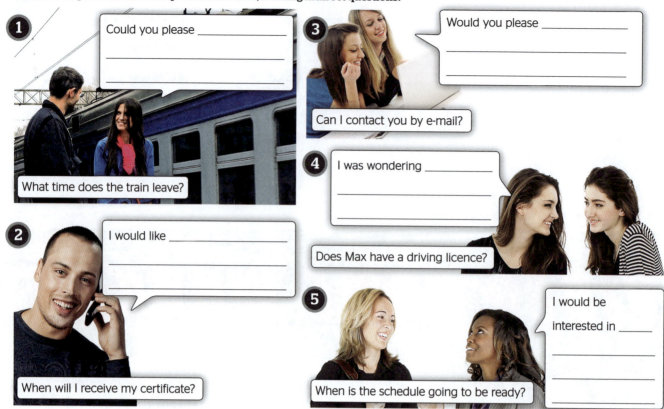

D. Read the e-mail below. The third paragraph is missing. Use the prompts to write the third paragraph. Form two indirect and two direct questions.

- cost
- stay with friend / in same host family
- lessons / available
- activities / offered

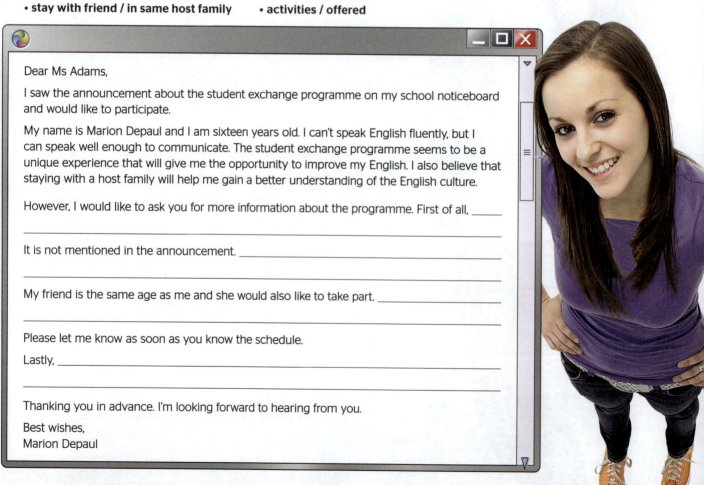

Student's Book pp. 82-83

A. Complete the sentences and do the crossword.

1. Gary is a(n) _____. He grows all sorts of vegetables.
2. My aunt is a brilliant _____. You should hear her play the piano.
3. Swimming is his favourite _____. Whenever he has some spare time, he goes swimming.
4. They may have won the _____ but they haven't won the war.
5. My team won the _____ by beating another local team in the final.
6. At the end of the story, the _____ is caught and punished.
7. My brother is a computer _____. I'm sure he can fix your laptop.

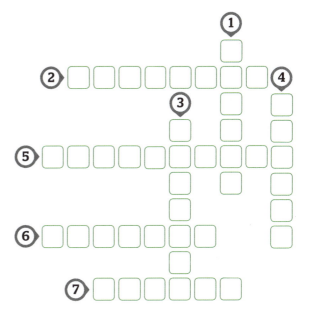

B. Complete the sentences with the correct prepositions.

1. You can count _____ me. I'll help you with the housework.
2. She can't take control _____ the situation. She needs our help.
3. I'm going to a jazz concert tomorrow. You know my passion _____ jazz.
4. Social networking sites help you hook up _____ people from around the world.
5. Beth ran _____ an old friend from school the other day.
6. Sam enjoys trying _____ new things.
7. It took John and Susan five years to build _____ their business.
8. I can't stand Daniela. She's always showing _____.

C. Circle the correct word.

1. We enjoyed our walk in the field **in spite of / although** the cold.
2. **Even though / Despite** she apologised, he didn't forgive her.
3. I joined the gym **so as to / although** lose some weight.
4. She played the piano **such / so** well that we were all very impressed.
5. They ran to the station **in order not to / so that** miss the train.
6. His report had **so / such** a lot of mistakes that he had to write it again.
7. **In spite of / Although** being very tired, she went out last night.
8. We gave them a map **despite / so that** they wouldn't get lost.
9. He is **such / so** a popular superhero that all the children love him.

6b

D. Complete the second sentence so that it has the same meaning as the first sentence, using the word given. Do not change the word given. You must use between two and five words including the word given.

1. Bob studies really hard, because he wants to get into a good university. **order**

   Bob studies really hard, _____ get into a good university.

2. Although she had all the necessary qualifications, she didn't get the job. **despite**

   She didn't get the job _____ all the necessary qualifications.

3. It was hot, but we didn't go for a swim. **though**

   Even _____, we didn't go for a swim.

4. There was a lot of noise, so I couldn't sleep. **much**

   There was _____ I couldn't sleep.

5. Despite her headache, she went to the cinema. **had**

   She went to the cinema _____ a headache.

6. Liam wants to sell his guitar and buy a new one. **as**

   Liam wants to sell his guitar _____ buy a new one.

7. The puzzle was so difficult that I couldn't do it. **such**

   It was _____ that I couldn't do it.

▶ Student's Book pp. 84-85

A. Choose a, b, c or d.

1. Information about the charity bike race is on the noticeboard for anyone who wants to take _____.
   a. place   b. part   c. control   d. time

2. I don't know the actor's name but he _____ in a TV programme about a man who worked for a fashion magazine.
   a. presented   b. starred   c. viewed   d. filmed

3. My parents are always there for me and I just take them for _____.
   a. seriously   b. time   c. sure   d. granted

4. If I watch four hours of TV every day, does that make me a TV _____?
   a. addict   b. channel   c. control   d. viewer

5. Harry's been working really hard lately so he's thinking about taking some time _____.
   a. on   b. over   c. in   d. off

6. Do you think it's _____ to bring my dog to the party?
   a. informative   b. unpopular   c. inappropriate   d. unlikely

B. Match. Then use to complete the sentences.

1. award — a. opera
2. remote — b. control
3. weather — c. guide
4. soap — d. TV
5. chat — e. ceremony
6. satellite — f. show
7. TV — g. forecast

1. Didn't you see the _____? You should take an umbrella with you.
2. I'm going to change the channel. Could you pass me the _____?
3. I don't understand why people watch this _____. The stories are so unbelievable.
4. Kevin's got _____ so he can choose from hundreds of channels.
5. It was announced that the _____ will take place at the Grand Theatre.
6. The _____ says the film begins at 8:00. But it's 8:15 and it still hasn't started.
7. I don't know why this woman is being interviewed on a _____. She isn't famous at all.

C. Complete the dialogue with the sentences in the box.

a. Don't take him seriously.
b. Take your time.
c. I can't take it any more.
d. Take it easy.
e. It'll help take your mind off things.

A: That's the last time I'm going anywhere with Fred! He's so annoying. **(1)** _____
B: What's he done now?
A: He was making fun of my new jacket all day.
B: He just likes to wind people up. **(2)** _____
A: I try not to. But sometimes he really winds me up! I'm never going to go anywhere with him again.
B: **(3)** _____ You're best friends. There's no need to fight over such a silly thing.
A: Maybe you're right.
B: Hey, let's relax and play some computer games. **(4)** _____
A: That's a good idea. But I have to make a phone call first.
B: No problem. **(5)** _____ I'll practise while I'm waiting.

▶▶ Student's Book pp. 86-87

A. Complete the paragraph with the correct form of the words in capitals.

I'm not a theatre lover, but last week I watched a very interesting play. It was a modern version of Shakespeare's *King Lear* by an exciting new **(1)** _____. The main plot is the same; a father decides to divide his kingdom among his three daughters, giving the largest piece to the one who loves him the most. The rest of the story is quite different without losing any emotion or suspense. As for the cast, both the leading actors and the **(2)** _____ cast were good. But what I found superb, was the **(3)** _____ of the actor playing King Lear. It's worth watching the play just for him. The costumes were probably the only **(4)** _____ because they were too simple and lacked imagination. All in all, it's a play which keeps you on the edge of your seat from the very beginning to the final curtain. It's full of action, plus it has a(n) **(5)** _____ ending which really shocked me. Also, this version of *King Lear* is less **(6)** _____ than the original, which may appeal to some people.

DIRECT
SUPPORT
PERFORM
DISAPPOINT
PREDICT
VIOLENCE

B. Complete the sentences with the words in the box.

villain   heroine

1. Jane Eyre in Charlotte Bronte's novel is a classic _____ loved by many readers.
2. The main bad character in a film is called the _____.

soundtrack   special effects

3. *Mission: Impossible Ghost Protocol* has got spectacular _____.
4. The _____ of this film is really good. You should listen to it.

blockbuster   box-office

5. I didn't like the film although it's this season's _____.
6. The *Titanic* was one of the biggest _____ hits of all time.

review   trailer

7. Have you seen the _____ for the latest David Lynch film?
8. According to this _____, this film is worth watching.

C. Match 1-6 with a-f to form sentences.

1. I was highly disappointed by the film because of
2. This is an excellent film, which
3. The special effects are impressive though
4. The film is suitable for adults, as well as
5. This is a great film, in which
6. Children should not watch this film because

a. Brad Pitt gives an amazing performance.
b. the terrible ending.
c. children.
d. it includes some very violent scenes.
e. everyone will love.
f. they are quite unrealistic.

D. Below is part of a film review on *Clash of the Titans*. The first and the third paragraphs are missing. Use the information given to complete the review. Also, use a variety of adjectives when making comments about the film (spectacular, disappointing, etc.)

Title: Clash of the Titans

Type of film: Fantasy / action

Director: Louis Leterrier

Leading actors: Sam Worthington (Perseus)
Liam Neeson (Zeus)
Ralph Fiennes (Hades)

	EXCELLENT	GOOD	NOT GOOD
plot			✔
acting			✔
special effects	✔		
costumes		✔	
ending	✔		
soundtrack	✔		

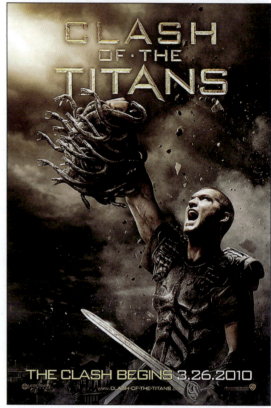

CLASH OF THE TITANS

_____
_____
_____
_____

The film is set in mythological Greece where a war between humans and gods is about to explode. The plot follows the life of Perseus and his battles with mythical beasts. Hades, the god of the underworld, warns that the city of Argos will be destroyed by a huge beast called the Kraken. When it is revealed to Perseus that he is half man and half god and his father is Zeus, he sets off on a journey with Argos' finest soldiers to find the Kraken.

_____
_____
_____
_____

All in all, I found *Clash of the Titans* very interesting and exciting because it helps you learn about mythology. It is a great choice for action-lovers.

6 Round-up

A. Complete the blanks with one word only.

I was walking along when a couple (1) _____ boys my age jumped right over my head. They were moving (2) _____ fast I didn't see where they had come from, or where they went. I found out they were doing parkour and they (3) _____ known as traceurs. I thought they were cool and I was really impressed. A month later an announcement (4) _____ made at my school that I was really excited about. Parkour would (5) _____ taught at our school after classes had finished on Tuesdays and Thursdays. I was thrilled and went to the shopping centre the next day in (6) _____ to buy a brand (7) _____ pair of trainers. The lessons were great and I learnt loads of moves. In the beginning, I wasn't sure I could cope (8) _____ the physical demands of parkour, but after a while I became much stronger. Now I practise all day in the garden and sometimes in my bedroom, which gets (9) _____ my parents' nerves a bit. It's become really popular with the whole school. After all, it's (10) _____ an exciting sport.

B. Complete the blanks with the correct form of the words in bold.

Looking for a fun and exciting gift? Each week, we suggest a different (1) _____ gift to give to your loved one. This week our (2) _____ is to become a DJ for a day (+ night). You don't have to be a (3) _____ or have any previous DJ experience. But a sense of rhythm is a (4) _____. There will be an extensive (5) _____ at a top recording studio. You will be allowed to use some of the most up-to-date equipment in the business. Meals and (6) _____ will be provided throughout the day. In the evening, you will visit a top London venue to show off your skills. Your (7) _____ will be judged by the people dancing at the venue. And if you're good enough, there's a (8) _____ you'll be asked back to DJ again. The (9) _____ of this gift is huge. So we suggest you book now if you want to give the gift within the next few months.

ACTIVE
RECOMMEND
MUSIC
NECESSARY
DEMONSTRATE
REFRESH
PERFORM
POSSIBLE
POPULAR

C. Choose a, b, c or d.

1. A documentary about the increasing environmental problems in our country _____ last night.
   a. were broadcast
   b. should be broadcast
   c. was broadcast
   d. had been broadcast

2. I fell asleep after I put the chicken in the oven so it was _____ .
   a. overslept
   b. overturned
   c. overcooked
   d. overtaken

3. There were _____ supporters at the football match that the noise was incredible.
   a. such
   b. so
   c. such a lot
   d. so many

4. There were more competitors than expected so the race had to take _____ at a larger park.
   a. part
   b. time
   c. place
   d. through

5. _____ of reading the whole book, Brad couldn't remember the name of the main character.
   a. Despite
   b. Even though
   c. Although
   d. In spite

6. My mum calls me a TV _____ because she thinks I watch too much TV.
   a. viewer
   b. addict
   c. guide
   d. show

7. I saved all my work onto my USB flash drive so _____ not to lose anything.
   a. as
   b. for
   c. that
   d. of

8. Anthony left his job because he couldn't cope _____ the pressure.
   a. from
   b. on
   c. with
   d. for

9. Roy and Dorian had created a terrible mess in the garden so they _____ clean it up.
   a. were made to
   b. were made
   c. made
   d. made to

10. I need peace and quiet to really concentrate _____ my homework.
    a. from
    b. on
    c. with
    d. for

D. Read the four texts about youth clubs below and answer the questions.

A. THE ONE CLUB

This is THE place to be if you're looking for fun and entertainment. You can join one of our many classes or just turn up and take it easy. It's up to you. Membership is free and every time you visit, you only have to pay €3. Every day we have a variety of fun activities from arts and crafts to video games, and at the weekend we organise football matches and table tennis tournaments. And don't forget, if you're really hungry on a Sunday afternoon, come down and enjoy some food from our delicious BBQ! All ages are welcome, so what are you waiting for?

B. TEEN CLUB

Are you looking for a place to hang out with your friends? Well, look no further. We have many activities including sports, video games, arts and crafts. We also have a full schedule of classes where you can learn parkour, karate, judo and taekwondo. There is also a canteen full of delicious snacks and a film room where you can grab a box of popcorn and check out the latest blockbuster. You don't have to pay to become a member. The only restriction we have is you have to be a teenager. Looking for fun? *Teen Club* is the place!

C. JUST 4 YOUTH

When your homework's done and you've got some free time, you need somewhere to have some fun. Well, *Just 4 Youth* has got it all! All the fun and exciting activities you'd expect from a youth club, and a whole lot more. Sign up today and get the chance to play sports, learn a new craft, or just come and use one of our many computers to surf the Net. Kids of all ages are welcome and membership only costs €35. But every visit is free of charge after that. You can also bring a friend along for a small fee of €2. There's so much to do, you'll be amazed! And if you just want to have a quiet place to finish your History or Maths project before the fun begins, we've got that too! See you there!

D. BELL PARK YOUTH CLUB

Bell Park Youth Club has been around for more than twenty years now. It's still the most popular youth club in the area. It's also the cheapest around, at only €2 per visit. All the usual activities are available, and you can now enjoy our brand new sports hall, perfect for volleyball, basketball and indoor football. Our old gym is now being used for dance classes, so if you want to try out ballet, or even want to be a b-boy or b-girl, you know where to come!

Which youth club...

1. do you have to be 13 and over to join?
2. only has sports on specific days?
3. charges people to become members?
4. has a special section where you can do your homework?
5. has a variety of martial arts classes?
6. serves grilled food on a particular day?
7. has improved its facilities recently?
8. has a place where you can watch films?

7a

▶▶ Student's Book pp. 90-91

A. Complete the sentences with the phrases in the box.

> back to nature   second nature   human nature   in my nature   good-natured   forces of nature

1. Taking photographs comes as _____ to David because he has been a photographer for 30 years.
2. Tim gets into trouble quite a lot, but deep down he's a _____ boy.
3. Many of my friends want to go _____ but I love living in London.
4. Don't be embarrassed about crying; it's only _____ to be upset when your pet dies.
5. Paul left his bike outside all winter and it was damaged by the _____.
6. Some people say that to be successful you have to forget about other people's feelings, but I don't agree. It's not _____.

B. Choose a, b, c or d.

Octopuses live all over the ocean, from (1) _____ waters to the deep ocean floor. They are fascinating creatures that can squeeze into extremely tight cracks, shoot out ink and even lose an arm when under attack, only to (2) _____ from it later by growing a new one. However, most people wouldn't consider them to be very (3) _____. It's true that octopuses have very small brains, but (4) _____, in scientific experiments they show (5) _____ intelligence. They nearly always end (6) _____ completing problem-solving activities proving that they have good short and long-term memory. Octopuses have also been known to use tools and are the only invertebrates (animals without bones) to (7) _____ tasks in this way. Some octopuses (8) _____ coconut shells to make a shelter. The intelligence of a particular German octopus called Paul, was put to the test during the World Cup in 2010. By choosing between two boxes of food with national flags on them, he was able (9) _____ the winner of each of the German national football team's seven matches, as well as the winner of the final. Obviously, this doesn't mean he was intelligent, just very lucky.

1. a. sanctuary	b. free	c. odd	d. shallow
2. a. give up	b. recover	c. get stuck	d. gather
3. a. loyal	b. devoted	c. smart	d. wisdom
4. a. somehow	b. somewhere	c. something	d. someone
5. a. necessary	b. extreme	c. extraordinary	d. smart
6. a. on	b. about	c. in	d. up
7. a. accomplish	b. gather	c. recover	d. present
8. a. run over	b. reveal	c. put	d. gather
9. a. predict	b. predicting	c. to predict	d. to predicting

7a

C. Circle the correct words.

Andy Come on, let's go.
Barry Go where?
Andy I've arranged (1) **to meet / meeting** Neal and Mark at the fast food place. Don't you remember?
Barry Hmmm. Why don't we stay at home? I've got a new video game.
Andy No, I'd rather (2) **go / going** out to eat. Anyway, you promised (3) **to come / come**. I hate it when you cancel at the last minute.
Barry OK, OK, I'll come. Just stop (4) **to complain / complaining**.
Andy You know what? I don't feel like (5) **to wait / waiting** for you to get ready. You can (6) **to stay / stay** at home and (7) **to play / play** your silly video games.
Barry Wait, I'm hungry. I want (8) **to have / have** something to eat.
Andy Well, get ready quickly, then…

D. Choose a, b or c.

1. Do you remember _____ that huge flock of birds in the park last year?
   a. see   **b.** seeing   **c.** to see
2. Try to avoid _____ your scraps on the floor. It makes such a mess.
   a. throwing   **b.** to throw   **c.** throw
3. There's no point in _____ that old bread as bait. The fish won't bite.
   a. to use   **b.** use   **c.** using
4. Nina advised her sister _____ away from the herd of cows.
   a. stay   **b.** to stay   **c.** staying
5. This cake is too sweet for me _____.
   a. to eat   **b.** eat   **c.** eating
6. Is it warm enough _____ in the sea today?
   a. swim   **b.** to swim   **c.** swimming
7. Dean was driving home when he stopped _____ a picture of a crow on a sign post.
   a. take   **b.** to take   **c.** taking
8. That man was hunting in the bird sanctuary, so you should _____ him to the authorities.
   a. reporting   **b.** to report   **c.** report

E. Complete the sentences with the correct form of the verb in brackets.

1. Paul likes _____ (play) chess with his father in his spare time.
2. I'm looking forward to _____ (see) my cousin again after so long.
3. James was really happy _____ (hear) that his sister was having a baby.
4. Mary had difficulty in _____ (find) curtains to match her sofa.
5. I borrowed my brother's jacket without _____ (ask) and now he's angry.
6. Does your mum let you _____ (watch) horror films?
7. I'll never forget _____ (win) the competition.
8. When you decide _____ (visit) the museum, remember _____ (go) to the gift shop.
9. Julian always helps his father _____ (wash) the car.
10. The teacher made the students _____ (sit) in silence.

▶▶ Student's Book pp. 92-93

A. Complete the sentences with the correct prepositions.

1. You've been coughing all day. Are you sure you're not coming down _____ something?
2. I'll come round your house and pick you _____ in about an hour.
3. They offered me the job, but I turned it _____.
4. Did you really see Lionel Messi on the underground, or are you just making it _____?
5. I really need to cut _____ on junk food. I can't fit into my trousers any more.
6. Ian and Roxy were an hour late because their car broke _____ on the way to the vet.
7. Don't use _____ all the milk. I need some for a cake I want to make.

B. Complete the sentences with the words in the box. You can use some of the words more than once. Then match the sentences with the correct picture.

> school   pack   swarm   herd   flock

1. I had to run inside because a _____ of bees suddenly appeared in the garden.
2. I had a horrible nightmare last night. I was walking in the forest when a _____ of wolves started chasing me.
3. Let's keep our distance from that _____ of cows so we don't disturb them.
4. We were on a cruise around the Caribbean when a _____ of dolphins started following the ship.
5. First we saw a farmer, then a huge _____ of sheep crossed the road.
6. There was a large _____ of deer at the zoo.
7. We sat on the hill and watched a _____ of goats passing by.
8. There was a _____ of ants moving a leaf outside my window.

C. Complete the sentences with the prepositional phrases in the box. There are two extra phrases you do not need to use.

> at the latest   at once   at the age of   at the end   at the beginning   at present   at last   at least   at first sight

1. Pablo Picasso died in 1973 _____ ninety-one.
2. I've finished my project on dolphins _____. It took me ages!
3. It's going to be hot tomorrow, so we'll need _____ two bottles of water.
4. The film starts at nine so meet me outside the cinema at 8:45 _____.
5. Don't forget to give me your test papers _____ of the exam.
6. Sally doesn't have a job _____, but she is hopeful that she'll find one by the end of the month.
7. There has been a tsunami warning! We must move away from the beach _____!

7a

D. Circle the correct words.

1. I've received **such / what** a lot of e-mails today!
2. **A:** Elaine's got a new pet dog called Rusty.
   B: How / So nice!
3. This chocolate cake is **such / so** delicious! You're a great cook.
4. We had **such / what** a great time at *Mario's* last Sunday.
5. I spent twenty euros to see that exhibition. **How / What** a waste of money!
6. **A:** Look at this view.
   B: What / How beautiful!
7. Mark is **what / so** embarrassing sometimes.
8. She's great. **So / How** wonderfully she dances!

E. Look at the pictures and write an exclamatory sentence for each situation. Use the adjective given.

1. (terrible)
   There's been a car accident.
   How _____!

2. (colourful)
   It's such _____!

3. (fast)
   That horse _____!

4. (scary)
   What _____!

5. (expensive)
   This is such _____!

6. (long)
   That lemur's tail _____!

▶▶ Student's Book pp. 94-95

A. Complete the text with the correct form of the words in capitals.

In 1995, Sangduen "Lek" Chailert from Thailand did something (1) _____ **WONDER**
to protect endangered elephants. She set up a sanctuary for the animals to live in a
(2) _____ natural environment. The Elephant Nature Park in Chiang Mai, in northern **PEACE**
Thailand, is located in an area surrounded by beautiful, (3) _____ landscape and **MOUNTAIN**
(4) _____ forests. Visitors come from all over the world to see this **TROPIC**
(5) _____ project. They come into contact with the rescued elephants and see how **IMPRESS**
(6) _____ the park is to them. The park aims to give visitors a **BENEFIT**
(7) _____ educational experience, teaching them about nature and the problems **VALUE**
faced by endangered species. The park also works to protect the (8) _____ values **CULTURE**
of the local community and employs local people to run the project. Lek has succeeded in creating a
(9) _____ tourist attraction that is doing extraordinary work for elephants and the **DELIGHT**
environment at the same time.

B. Choose a, b, c or d.

1. Some people find going for long walks _____ but I really enjoy being outdoors.
   a. astonishing   b. dull   c. energising   d. inviting
2. I was very lucky to grow up in the _____, away from the pressures of life in the city.
   a. coast   b. waterfall   c. countryside   d. valley
3. The new five star hotel offers _____ accommodation to guests, but at an extremely high price.
   a. cute   b. luxurious   c. overwhelmed   d. truly
4. Many people who have stressful jobs try to book a holiday at least once a year so that they can escape _____ their routine.
   a. from   b. with   c. off   d. away
5. Well, if you don't believe me, come and see _____ yourself.
   a. by   b. for   c. with   d. at

C. Read the description of a place and write a catchy title. Then complete the text with rhetorical questions.

_____

_____

You can go to Longleat Safari and Adventure Park in the south-west of England and experience the thrill of seeing many different wild animals. I was lucky enough to go there last summer. It was a nice experience, one that I will never forget.

Longleat opened in 1966 and was the first safari park outside of Africa. It is located in the nice Wiltshire countryside and visitors can drive through various animal areas such as the 'Lion Country' and 'Tiger Territory'. You can also see nice animals like zebras, wolves, elephants and even giraffes there. More importantly, it is now home to all sorts of endangered animals.

Apart from seeing all these animals, you can also come into close contact with them. For example, we drove through the park and at one point a group of monkeys jumped on top of our car! It was quite a surprise, but a nice experience. After seeing the monkeys, we visited a cave full of bats. There were so many that we were absolutely surrounded by them!

There were so many nice things to see and do at Longleat that we could have spent three days there! _____

_____ It's truly a nice experience!

D. Look at the text again and replace *nice* with the adjectives in the box. There is more than one possible answer in each case. Wherever necessary, replace the article *a* with *an*.

amazing   marvellous   great   wonderful   exciting   unforgettable

Student's Book pp. 96-97

A. Circle the correct words.

1. We need to get **rid / dispose** of all the old furniture that has been stored in the garage.
2. It is now well-known that smoking has many bad **affects / effects** on your health.
3. Great! I killed two birds with one **device / stone**.
4. If you travel **frequently / particularly**, many airline companies will offer you discounts on future flights.
5. A new shop has opened that sells building and DIY **materials / junk**.
6. Fortunately, she wasn't hurt but she shouldn't have been there in the first **case / place**.

B. Complete the sentences with the correct form of the words in capitals.

1. There are many ways to _____ plastic. For example, plastic food pots can be used again in the garden for plants. **USE**
2. Supermarkets have been asking _____ to use their plastic bags more than once to help the environment. **CONSUME**
3. There are many charity shops in London that collect people's _____ clothes and sell them to raise money for good causes. **WANTED**
4. The articles written by different _____ showed the very serious dangers of global warming. **RESEARCH**
5. Many people do not know how much of our everyday rubbish is actually _____. **RECYCLE**

C. Read the dialogues and circle the correct words.

1. **A:** I can't find my books anywhere!
   B: Did you ask Lara? She **might borrow / might have borrowed** them.
2. Which hotel did you stay at when you went to London?
   We **didn't need to book / needn't have booked** a hotel room. We stayed at my aunt's house.
3. **A:** Becky went shopping yesterday.
   B: She **can't have gone / shouldn't have gone**. It was a holiday and all the shops were closed.
4. **A:** This coffee tastes horrible!
   B: Oh no! I **could have put / must have put** salt instead of sugar in it!
5. **A:** I can't believe I failed my Biology exam!
   B: I'm not surprised. You **should have studied / must have studied** more!
6. **A:** Did you go to the concert last night?
   B. Yes, but I didn't enjoy it. I **may have stayed / 'd rather have stayed** at home.

D. Complete the second sentence so that it has a similar meaning to the first, using the word given. Do not change the word given. You must use between two and five words including the word given.

1. You were lucky that you didn't crash into the tree. **could**
   You were lucky, because you _____ into the tree.
2. It is certain that they knew about the new project. **must**
   They _____ about the new project.
3. It was not a good idea to leave the cat alone for three days. **should**
   You _____ the cat alone for three days.

4. Dan is late, so it's possible that his car broke down again.

Dan is late, so _____ down again.

might

5. It isn't possible that she saw Bill yesterday. He was at work until very late.

She _____ Bill yesterday. He was at work until very late.

have

6. It wasn't necessary for you to buy me a birthday present.

You _____ me a birthday present.

need

▶▶ Student's Book pp. 98-99

A. Match. Then complete the sentences.

1. acid — a. fuels
2. oil — b. spill
3. toxic — c. energy
4. fossil — d. food
5. alternative — e. fumes
6. exhaust — f. rain
7. organic — g. waste

1. A tanker crashed into the rocks near the coast creating a huge _____.
2. With _____ running out so fast, we need to develop _____ if we want to survive as a species.
3. With so much traffic in the city, the amount of _____ is becoming a huge problem.
4. I try not to shop at that supermarket because they don't sell _____.
5. The fish are dying because of the _____ that factories are pumping into the rivers.
6. This statue should be put in a museum and not left outside to be destroyed by _____.

B. Choose a, b, c or d.

ECO

An environmental organisation called *Eco-world*, is running a competition for schools in Ireland to raise environmental awareness. The school which proves to be the most environmentally aware will win €2000.

Entries so far have included a project showing how difficult it is to (1) _____ the air in many cities because of all the pollution in the (2) _____. Another school has created an experiment which shows how (3) _____ and fog combine to make smog. There are also recommendations on how to deal with all the (4) _____ people leave lying around in the streets. Some schools are choosing specific problems and are even getting active. For example, Mountbatton School is insisting that a factory in their area should be closed (5) _____, because of the amount of chemicals that are being (6) _____ into a nearby lake.

It's encouraging to see young students getting involved and helping to protect the environment.

1. a. last   b. live   c. breathe   d. form
2. a. fog   b. atmosphere   c. surface   d. substance
3. a. gas   b. coal   c. fuel   d. smoke
4. a. chemicals   b. fumes   c. litter   d. substance
5. a. up   b. in   c. out   d. down
6. a. banned   b. pumped   c. fined   d. biodegraded

7b

▶▶ Student's Book pp. 100-101

A. Complete the sentences with the correct form of the words in capitals.

1. The young photographer showed his photos to the _____ of the newspaper who was very impressed. **EDIT**
2. Do you really think that this is _____ behaviour for a person in his late teens? **ACCEPT**
3. The police arrested eleven _____ who had made an illegal camp on private land. **PROTEST**
4. Tomorrow we're going on a _____ to stop a factory from being built at the edge of our town. **DEMONSTRATE**

B. Complete the sentences with the correct prepositions.

1. I'd like to point _____ that building a skatepark next to a main road is a bad idea.
2. According _____ my science teacher, even organic food has some amount of chemicals in it.
3. In response _____ your last comment, I disagree with you that people prefer to use public transport than drive.
4. The government says they will create more job opportunities _____ all costs.
5. Should we still go ahead _____ the picnic even though it looks like it's going to rain?

C. Complete the text with the words in the box. There are two extra words which you do not need to use.

| dustmen | outrageous | mayor | concerned | survey | article | source | growing | held |

Yesterday afternoon the (1) _____ of Kindleford, John Ruskin, spoke to some residents at a meeting which was (2) _____ at the town hall. He talked about his plans for the development of the town. He had been criticised recently in a(n) (3) _____ in the local newspaper and wanted to set things straight. The article reported the results of a(n) (4) _____ which showed how he had abandoned Kindleford and done very little to improve the quality of life there, which Ruskin described as (5) _____.

He also spoke about the (6) _____ problem of rubbish in the town. However, he didn't offer a single solution to the problem. There were a few (7) _____ present at the meeting who wanted to speak out. After they explained how difficult their jobs were, Ruskin promised to do whatever he could to help them.

D. Read the writing task below and use the ideas to complete the mind map.

You read this article in a local newspaper. Write a letter to the editor expressing your views.

A major environmental issue our city is facing is pollution. This problem has been getting worse and worse over the past ten years and residents are asking the authorities to come up with acceptable solutions to solve the problem. One solution is to introduce a system of carpooling where people would share a car with other people on regular journeys instead of driving alone. Is it a good idea? Write to us and tell us what you think.

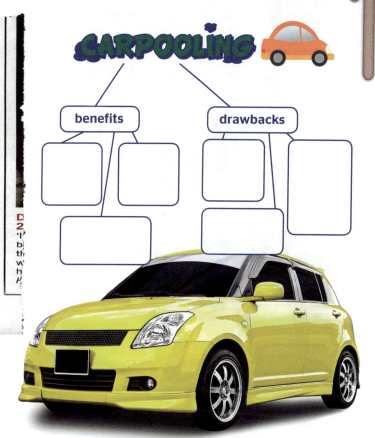

Think about
- the traffic
- the pollution
- how easy it is to find people to travel with
- the time needed to pick up people and drop them off
- the money spent on petrol
- the privacy you have

E. Use the mind map to write the missing paragraphs.

Dear Sir/Madam,

I'm writing in response to an article I recently read in your newspaper about carpooling. I was very interested to read about this solution to the problem of pollution in our city and I would like to express my views on the topic.

First of all, _____

_____

_____

_____

_____

_____

On the other hand, _____

_____

_____

_____

_____

_____

In conclusion, I do not think the disadvantages are serious, so I believe that introducing the system of carpooling is a wonderful idea.

Yours faithfully,

Peter Costner

Peter Costner

7 Round-up

A. Complete the text with the correct form of the words in capitals.

Malbork is a small (1) _____ town in northern Poland. Although Malbork is an (2) _____ and pleasant place to visit, it isn't a (3) _____ famous town. However, it does have one claim to fame. Malbork Castle, which is in the town, is the largest castle in the world by area. Construction of the castle started in 1274 and an (4) _____ 232 years later, the castle was completed. It is located on the river Nogat, which was (5) _____ for access and trade, and its size made it the perfect place for Medieval Kings to live a (6) _____ lifestyle. Today the castle is as (7) _____ as it was when it was built. It attracts many visitors and it is a very important (8) _____ site. There is a fascinating museum in the castle which holds many (9) _____ treasures from the castle's long history. If you're ever in Poland and you're looking for an (10) _____ place to go, then Malbork is definitely worth a visit.

PEACE
ENJOY
PARTICULAR

ASTONISH

BENEFIT
LUXURY
IMPRESS

CULTURE
VALUE

FORGET

B. Choose a, b, c or d.

1. The dogs ran into the field and started chasing a _____ of sheep.
   a. herd   b. flock   c. pack   d. swarm
2. It was only later that we discovered that James had _____ up the whole story.
   a. turned   b. given   c. ended   d. made
3. Dave found a lot of old _____ at the back of his cupboard. But he didn't know whether to throw it away or not.
   a. junk   b. waste   c. rubbish   d. litter
4. Cutting down the forest will destroy the _____ habitat of many animals.
   a. coastal   b. natural   c. cultural   d. atmosphere
5. Karina has given _____ trying to teach Alice Russian.
   a. out   b. up   c. down   d. over

C. Choose a, b or c.

1. I don't know which handbag _____ with me to the theatre tonight.
   a. take   b. taking   c. to take
2. The oil spill was _____ bad! Thousands of sea birds died.
   a. such   b. how   c. so
3. A: I left a bag of clothes here and went inside. Now it's gone!
   B: The dustmen _____ it.
   a. must have taken   b. should have taken   c. would have taken
4. Ronda is thinking of _____ the bird sanctuary tomorrow afternoon.
   a. to visit   b. visiting   c. visit
5. _____ amazing animals you can find at the zoo!
   a. How   b. What   c. Such
6. You _____ a school of whales, because they don't exist in this part of the sea.
   a. shouldn't have seen   b. needn't have seen   c. can't have seen
7. You should _____ of those batteries properly, you know.
   a. dispose   b. disposing   c. to dispose
8. The Knock Nevis was _____ a large tanker! It took over five miles to come to a stop.
   a. so   b. how   c. such

D. Read the text and complete it with the missing sentences a-g. There is one sentence which you do not need to use.

a. We are lucky to have trees and plants on the Earth which take in carbon dioxide and give off oxygen.
b. Leaders of countries from all over the world gather together to discuss environmental issues and suggest solutions to reduce global warming.
c. A typical greenhouse in a garden is made of glass which allows sunlight in, but prevents heat from escaping.
d. This is the main reason that the greenhouse effect causes global warming.
e. The rise in the planet's temperature will cause major changes in the weather around the world.
f. The main gases that create the atmosphere are carbon dioxide, methane and water.
g. Take the effort to recycle products, only use your car if you really need to, turn off the lights when you leave the room.

the GREENHOUSE EFFECT: What's it all about?

You've probably heard about the greenhouse effect during discussions on the environment. It may sound like something negative, but in actual fact, without the greenhouse effect there would be no life on Earth. **(1)** _____ This way, the temperature in a greenhouse can be warm even during winter.

The Earth's atmosphere works in the same way as a greenhouse. The atmosphere contains gases which trap the heat from the sun giving the Earth an average temperature of 15ºC which is suitable for life. **(2)** _____ The increase of carbon dioxide in the atmosphere is mainly caused by burning fossil fuels, by power stations, cars and planes, etc. The problem is that if the amount of greenhouse gases increases a lot, then the greenhouse effect is too strong. This leads to global warming, where the Earth becomes warmer and warmer, as is happening now. **(3)** _____ But instead of making sure there are more trees to cope with the increase of carbon dioxide, humans are destroying forests and making the problem worse.

The effects of global warming on the world are difficult to predict, but most scientists are very worried. **(4)** _____ On the one hand, many countries will suffer long periods of dry weather, making it difficult to farm land. On the other hand, the ice at the North and South Poles will begin to melt, causing sea levels to rise. All this will lead to extreme weather conditions such as tropical storms.

It is an issue that affects the whole world. That is why every five years, the United Nations organises the Earth Summit. **(5)** _____ These mainly include ways to cut down on the amount of carbon dioxide countries produce. But the use of alternative energy in the future is also discussed.

You may think that it is such a huge problem that whatever you do won't make a difference. But if everyone gets involved and starts thinking more about the environment, it won't take much to improve the situation. **(6)** _____ All of these will add up and could have a big impact on the future of our planet.

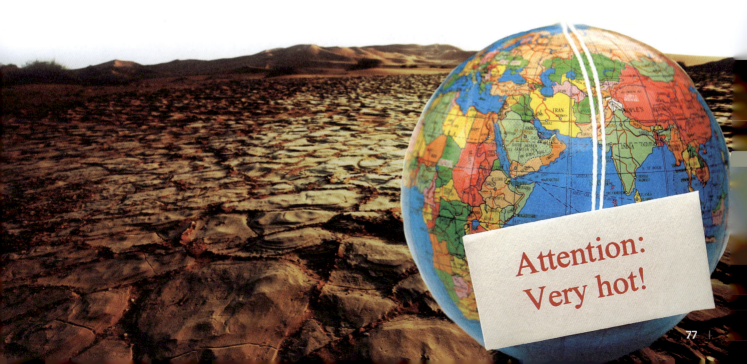

Attention: Very hot!

8a

>> **Student's Book pp. 104-105**

A. Complete the text with the words in the box. There are two extra words which you do not need to use.

> media   looks   truth   disapproves
> appreciates   genuine   portraits   edit

Hollywood actress Kate Winslet is one of the few celebrities who have spoken openly about how magazines use Photoshop to make them look perfect. She **(1)** _____ of this and feels that it is important to inform people that images in magazines bend the **(2)** _____. She said that she often looks very different in reality to how she is shown in photographs. It is very common for magazines to **(3)** _____ images and almost every famous person has probably been changed at least once in photographs. The **(4)** _____ has been blamed for putting a lot of pressure on young people, especially women, to think about their **(5)** _____ and to try and look like the celebrities they see. So keep in mind the images that are presented to us are not all **(6)** _____ and we must remember this when we see them. This is why it's very good that actresses like Kate Winslet remind the public that what they see is not always reality.

B. Tick (✔) the person / people responsible for the action described in each of the sentences below.

1. a. Brenda is typing her report.   Brenda ◯   somebody else ◯
   b. Brenda is having her report typed.   Brenda ◯   somebody else ◯

2. a. The Morris family will have a swimming pool put in their garden.   The Morris family ◯   somebody else ◯
   b. The Morris family will put a swimming pool in their garden.   The Morris family ◯   somebody else ◯

3. a. Harry repaired his motorbike.   Harry ◯   somebody else ◯
   b. Harry had his motorbike repaired.   Harry ◯   somebody else ◯

4. a. Kathy is having her kitchen cleaned.   Kathy ◯   somebody else ◯
   b. Kathy is cleaning her kitchen.   Kathy ◯   somebody else ◯

5. a. The mayor had a new park built in the centre.   The mayor ◯   somebody else ◯
   b. The mayor built a new park in the centre.   The mayor ◯   somebody else ◯

C. Rewrite the following sentences using the Causative Form.

1. The hairdresser cut Marianne's hair.

   Marianne _____

2. The gardener was planting flowers in my garden yesterday morning.

   I _____

3. Susan didn't decorate her house herself. She asked a decorator to do it.

   Susan _____

4. We will ask Mr Roberts to replace the broken window.

   We _____

5. I must ask a painter to paint the fence because I can't do it.

   I _____

D. Complete the dialogue with the causative form of the prompts in brackets.

Maggie So, Sonia, how has your life changed ever since you won the lottery?

Sonia Oh, it has become so much easier.

Maggie What do you mean?

Sonia Well, I don't have to do any housework any more. I (1) _____ (my house / clean) and (2) _____ (my clothes / wash) by Ms Marple. I don't cook any more either. I (3) _____ (my meals / cook) by Ms Marple, too. She's an excellent cook.

Maggie Really?

Sonia Of course! I also (4) _____ (my hair / style) every morning by the best hairdresser in town. And I often go shopping. I love buying new clothes and accessories. But I don't go to the supermarket because that's kind of boring. I (5) _____ (that / do) by Ms Marple, too.

Maggie You seem to be enjoying yourself. What will you do when you run out of money?

Sonia Well, I haven't really thought about that.

Maggie Maybe you should think about it and be ready to manage without the money that you have now.

▶▶ Student's Book pp. 106-107

A. Complete the text with the correct form of the words in capitals.

Many teenagers find it difficult to talk to their parents and complain that they are misunderstood. At the same time, though, parents worry that if their children sometimes (1) _____ or get used to being (2) _____, they will experience problems at school and later on in life.

However, teenage behaviour is often (3) _____, and usually there is nothing for parents to worry about. Teenagers naturally go through periods when they don't feel like talking to their parents. The list of reasons for this can be (4) _____, so it doesn't necessarily mean they are having serious problems. Parents should try not to (5) _____ their children and be patient with them if they sometimes (6) _____ them. It is normal for children to want to stand up to their parents as they get older, and it is not always a sign of (7) _____.

Young people need to have the space to express themselves and to know that their parents will not (8) _____. At the same time it is important for teenagers to help their parents understand them, because if there is no communication at all, teenagers might start to feel (9) _____.

Everyone needs to work together to make a happy family!

BEHAVE
ORGANISE
LEAD
END
JUDGE
OBEY
RESPECT
APPROVE
HELP

B. Circle the correct words.

1. Daisy really **did / made** a fashion statement when she wore that bright red hat to the party.
2. Andy fell over and broke his tooth and had to have a(n) **unreal / false** one fitted by the dentist.
3. Nicole is such a fashion **victim / material**. All she cares about is wearing clothes that are trendy, even if they don't suit her!
4. It is not **genuine / realistic** to say that we will finish the project by the end of the week. It's simply not possible.
5. Clothes that were trendy during the 1980s have recently **made / come** into fashion again.
6. When Rita bought her plane tickets online, she **misinformed / misspelt** her name and when she arrived at the airport, the official would not allow her on the flight.
7. After travelling in the car for two hours, the children became **restless / dissatisfied** and wanted to get out and play.

8a

C. Complete the second sentence so that it means the same as the first. Use no more than three words.

1. I wore a coat when I went outside, so I didn't get wet.

   If I _____ a coat when I went outside, I would have got wet.

2. Danny didn't drive you to the station, so you missed the train.

   If Danny had driven you to the station, you might _____ the train.

3. I didn't go out last night, so I didn't meet my friends.

   If I _____ last night, I would have met my friends.

4. They didn't see the sign, so they got lost.

   If they had seen the sign, they would _____ lost.

5. Fay couldn't call Sheila, because she didn't know her number.

   If Fay had known Sheila's number, she _____ her.

6. Billy didn't tidy his room, so his mother got angry.

   If Billy _____ his room, his mother would not have got angry.

7. Sheila fell asleep, so she burnt the food.

   If Sheila _____ asleep, she wouldn't have burnt the food.

8. Lucy didn't go to the concert, because she didn't have a ticket.

   If Lucy had bought a ticket, she would _____ to the concert.

D. Choose a, b, c or d.

1. If it _____ yesterday, we would have gone on a picnic.
   - **a.** had rained
   - **b.** hadn't rained
   - **c.** didn't rain
   - **d.** doesn't rain

2. If you _____ tennis, you shouldn't take it up.
   - **a.** didn't like
   - **b.** hadn't liked
   - **c.** don't like
   - **d.** wouldn't like

3. The house _____ during the earthquake if it had not been built so well.
   - **a.** would collapse
   - **b** will collapse
   - **c.** would have collapsed
   - **d.** collapsed

4. If Julie had planted roses in winter, the cold _____ them.
   - **a.** will destroy
   - **b.** can destroy
   - **c.** could destroy
   - **d.** could have destroyed

5. The team would have won the match if they _____ more.
   - **a.** practise
   - **b.** will practise
   - **c.** practised
   - **d.** had practised

6. Henry _____ down all the factories which pollute the city if he became mayor.
   - **a.** would close
   - **b.** will close
   - **c.** would have closed
   - **d.** could close

Student's Book pp. 108-109

A. Complete the sentence with the words in the box. There are two extra words which you do not need to use.

| addiction | dye | jealous | sensitive | insecure | rejected | reassured | shade |

1. Many people enjoy exercising so much that it becomes almost a(n) _____. A whole day without some kind of a workout seems out of the question.
2. Magazine publishers should remember that young people can be very _____ to the images that they see.
3. During the summer the colour of Lucy's hair is always a(n) _____ lighter.
4. The police _____ the woman that they would do everything they could to find the burglar.
5. When Tony's younger brother was born, he was sometimes _____ of him.
6. Alice felt _____ by her friends when she wasn't invited to Rita's house.

B. Complete the second sentence so that it has a similar meaning to the first sentence, using the word given. Do not change the word given. You must use between two and five words including the word given.

1. Andy is just like his father.
   Andy _____ his father. **after**
2. Oliver usually asks his cousin, who works at a bank, for financial advice.
   Whenever Oliver needs financial advice, he usually _____ his cousin, who works at a bank. **turns**
3. It took the children two hours to find a solution to their problem.
   After two hours the children _____ a solution to their problem. **out**
4. Frank supported his brother when he decided to change career even though he knew it would be difficult for him.
   Even though he knew it would be difficult for his brother, Frank _____ him when he decided to change career. **stood**
5. I really admire my uncle and would like to be like him when I grow up.
   I want to be like my uncle when I grow up because I really _____ him. **up**
6. Sophie was so sad when her cat died that she lost control and started crying.
   When Sophie's cat died she _____ completely. **broke**

C. Complete the sentences with the correct form of the words in capitals.

1. It is _____ that Jack got the job just because he knows the boss. **FAIR**
2. Those who are lucky enough to be _____ should help people who are in need. **WEALTH**
3. Ben had a cold and felt really _____ as he had to stay at home. **MISERY**
4. The teacher gave a _____ about ways to protect the environment. **PRESENT**
5. Images in magazines of beautiful models can make people feel _____ as they compare themselves to the models in the pictures. **SECURE**
6. Passing his driving test gave Jack a real sense of _____. **ACHIEVE**

8a

D. Complete the letter with the sentences a-d in the box.

a. Let me know how everything turns out.
b. I really don't think that you should end your friendship with Vivian over a misunderstanding.
c. I've given your problem a lot of thought and I've come up with a solution.
d. If I were you, I'd talk to Vivian about what happened.

Dear Anne,

I was sorry to hear that you've got a problem with Vivian. You two seemed to be very good friends. **(1)** _____

In your last letter, you wrote that Vivian embarrassed you in front of your classmates. Did it ever cross your mind that she didn't mean to embarrass you? **(2)** _____ I strongly advise you to give it more thought.

Perhaps she hasn't realised how much she's upset you. **(3)** _____ However, if you speak with her and she doesn't apologise, she's obviously not a true friend.

Well, I hope I've been of some help. **(4)** _____
Take care,
Susan

E. Look at the letter again. What advice does Susan give to Anne?

1. _____
2. _____

F. Rewrite Susan's suggestions by completing the sentences below.

1. Maybe you shouldn't _____
2. Why don't you _____

8b

▶▶ Student's Book pp. 110-111

A. Complete the sentences with the words in the box. There are two extra words which you do not need to use.

| represent   beside   puddle   aim   situated   concept   exhibited   criticised   melted   confused |

The Tate Modern is a modern art gallery **(1)** _____ in the centre of London. The building was originally a power station **(2)** _____ the Thames in the Bankside district of London. In 1993 a decision was made to destroy the building, but many people **(3)** _____ this decision and finally, in 1994 the Tate Gallery announced that the building would be the home of the new Tate Modern. The **(4)** _____ of the Tate Modern was to have a collection that would **(5)** _____ all the major modern art movements from the 1900s onwards. However, the Tate's organisation of artwork **(6)** _____ many visitors in the beginning because it is not **(7)** _____ in historical order, as with most museums. The works of art are arranged by themes like, Memory/History/Society. Despite this, people soon got used to the **(8)** _____ and today, the Tate Modern is one of the most visited galleries in the UK.

B. Choose a, b, c or d.

1. Noel entered the back of the crowded room quietly so he wouldn't draw attention _____ himself.
   a. for   b. to   c. about   d. on
2. Many people disliked the way the artist had _____ the centre of town into a huge rubbish bin.
   a. transformed   b. rejected   c. challenged   d. permitted
3. This gallery shop has a wide _____ of postcards and posters.
   a. aim   b. goal   c. range   d. desire
4. The main _____ for calling this meeting is to discuss the last day of school celebrations.
   a. purpose   b. concept   c. warning   d. sense
5. Roger hasn't sold any paintings yet, but a _____ of people have shown an interest.
   a. few   b. kind   c. result   d. number
6. Police received a(n) _____ phone call this morning explaining where to find the stolen jewels.
   a. rapid   b. anonymous   c. confusing   d. creative

C. Complete the sentences with the correct form of the words in capitals.

1. Eric's art teacher was impressed by his skill and _____. **CREATE**
2. Looking over the bridge, Elaine could see her _____ in the river below. **REFLECT**
3. Oliver is a _____ from Chicago who makes artwork out of plastic and wood. **SCULPT**
4. Everyone seems to be aware of _____ warming, but nobody is doing anything to help the situation. **GLOBE**
5. Police are investigating the _____ of the golden statue from the town square last week. **APPEARANCE**
6. This is a problem that not only affects the people of our country, but the whole of _____. **HUMAN**

D. Circle the correct words.

1. Bernie wishes he **had / had had** time to go to the bank yesterday.
2. My mother wishes we **wouldn't / couldn't** forget our keys all the time.
3. If only we **have / had** remembered to bring our scarves. It's freezing.
4. Mark wishes he **could / would** travel all over the world.
5. If only my brother **had been / were** here to help us right now!
6. I wish you **would / could** stop complaining about the weather.
7. If only Josie **would do / will do** something to improve her marks.
8. Jonathan wishes he **had / has** tickets to the basketball match.

E. Read the dialogues and complete with the correct form of the verbs in brackets.

1. **A:** We had a great time at the art gallery yesterday.
   B: Really? If only I _____ (come) with you.
2. **A:** Our Maths exam is tomorrow.
   B: Oh, no. If only I _____ (have) more time to study.
3. **A:** It looks like it's going to rain.
   B: You're right. I wish I _____ (take) my umbrella with me.
4. **A:** Do you want to go for a walk?
   B: Not really. I wish you _____ (let) me read my newspaper.
5. **A:** Hey, Katie! Your hoody is really cool!
   B: Mum! I wish you _____ (talk) like that. It's embarrassing.
6. **A:** I think you should buy that skirt. It would suit you.
   B: I wish I _____ (afford) it. I've only got €20.

8b

F. Read the situations and reply using *wish/if only*.

1. Jake didn't tell the truth earlier and now he's in trouble.
   _____

2. It's too bad that I don't know how to use a computer.
   _____

3. Chris regrets eating so many chocolates.
   _____

4. Sam can't speak Chinese so he couldn't understand many people while on his trip to China.
   _____

5. It would be better if Carol didn't interrupt me every five minutes.
   _____

▶▶ Student's Book pp. 112-113

A. Complete the crossword.

B. Complete the text with the words in the box.

| ring | pattern | jewellery | precious | pottery | origami | carved | crafts | clay | earrings |

My oldest sister was getting married, and I wanted to give her a special gift. I thought about getting her some (1) _____, but she has lots of bracelets and whenever I buy her (2) _____ she nearly always loses one of them. I'd also seen a(n) (3) _____ with a beautiful (4) _____ stone in it. But then, I realised I wanted the gift to be more personal, so I decided to use my arts and (5) _____ skills and make something for her. A nice sculpture (6) _____ out of wood would have been nice, but that would have taken ages. I'm also quite good at (7) _____ but I think a wedding gift made out of paper seems a bit too cheap. Finally, I decided to try doing some (8) _____ and make her a lovely fruit bowl. I thought of creating a nice (9) _____ using the first letters of her and her fiancé's names. I was very excited about the idea and rushed to the art shop to buy some (10) _____. However, it turned out to be a disaster. Every time I made something, it collapsed. In the end, I bought her a nice boring brooch. But I'm determined to make her something one day. So I'm going to join the local college and learn something new.

▶▶ Student's Book pp. 114-115

A. Complete the sentences with the words in the box. There are two extra words which you do not need to use.

| involvement | aspect | head teacher | considerably | carried out | forum |
| specifically | motivate | limit | stage | volunteered |

1. This report fails to mention the most important _____ of the problem.
2. Mr Jenkins was annoyed because most of his recommendations weren't _____.
3. The blue whale is _____ larger than other whales in the ocean.
4. I read about the celebrity's situation on an Internet _____, but I didn't believe a word of it.
5. Ms Bryson sent me to the _____ even though I had done nothing wrong.
6. Try to _____ your report to about 250 words.
7. Most of the school teachers realise how important it is to _____ students if you want them to learn.
8. During the final _____ of the biscuit making process, chocolate is poured on the top.
9. Edward has _____ to put up posters around the town.

8b

B. Write a heading above each paragraph of the report. Choose from the headings in the box. There is one extra heading which you do not need to use.

- Making the park greener
- Introduction
- Better organisation
- Conclusion
- Council involvement
- Attracting different ages

To: Glenda Ingles, Head of Parks commission
From: Andy Smith
Subject: Wimbledon Park

1. _____
The purpose of this report is to point out some negative aspects of Wimbledon Park and suggest how it can be improved.

2. _____
First of all, we need to take into consideration the fact that Wimbledon Park is one of the few areas in our town where people can go to relax and enjoy a bit of fresh air. However, the trees and plants in the park are not looked after properly and many of them have died or suffer from diseases. Therefore, it is recommended that more trees should be planted and more gardeners should be hired to take care of the park.

3. _____
Furthermore, a few simple arrangements need to be made so that the park can become a cleaner and more enjoyable place to visit. First of all, more rubbish bins should be placed throughout the park so that people will not throw their litter on the ground. Add to this a better pathway system, and people would find Wimbledon Park a nicer place to visit.

4. _____
Last but not least, Wimbledon Park should be a place for all the family to enjoy. At the moment, there is nothing to do there and so it is not very attractive. It is a large area of land which could be divided into areas with different activities. Moreover, a new safe playground should be built for younger visitors, whereas teenagers would definitely enjoy a skatepark. Also, tennis and basketball courts would appeal to more people and encourage them to stay fit and healthy.

5. _____
To sum up, I believe that if the above recommendations are carried out, Wimbledon Park will become a much more pleasant place to visit.

C. Read parts of various reports and rewrite the sentences using the Passive Voice.

1. This report focuses on what we should do to improve the gym at our school.
   _____

2. With these small changes, we will solve the majority of the problems.
   _____

3. In addition, we must update all the computers in the computer room.
   _____

4. Also, people have asked many questions about the government's involvement.
   _____

5. Finally, we will cause a lot more problems if we don't do anything about the situation.
   _____

8 Round-up

A. Complete the second sentence so that it has a similar meaning to the first sentence, using the word given. Do not change the word given. You must use between two and five words including the word given.

1. Jack had the support of his father through all the difficulties when he set up his new business. **stood**
   When Jack set up his new business, his father _____ through all the difficulties.

2. I want to lend you some money, but I haven't got much myself. **wish**
   I _____ you some money, but I haven't got much myself.

3. I didn't go on the school trip because I had a cold. **would**
   I _____ on the school trip if I hadn't had a cold.

4. She is going to the dentist this afternoon so that he can clean her teeth. **have**
   She is going to _____ by the dentist this afternoon.

5. Gemma didn't hear her phone ring so she missed the call. **would**
   Gemma _____ the call if she had heard her phone ring.

6. After a few hours the men calculated the cost of the project. **worked**
   The men _____ the cost of the project after a few hours.

7. The singer in the band has had an argument with the other members and has cancelled the concert. **fell**
   The singer in the band _____ the other members and has cancelled the concert.

B. Choose a, b, c or d.

How much do we judge people by their **(1)** _____? An experiment carried **(2)** _____ by a newspaper in the United States has proved that we are often **(3)** _____ by a person's appearance. On a morning in January 2007 at one of Washington's busiest metro stations, where a(n) **(4)** _____ number of people were on their way to work, a man dressed in casual clothes picked up his violin and started playing. The **(5)** _____ of the people in the station continued walking and took no notice **(6)** _____ him and the music he was playing. If only they **(7)** _____ that the musician was Joshua Bell, one of the world's best violinists, playing some of the most difficult music ever written, on a hand-made violin worth over $3.5 million! One of the few people who **(8)** _____ the music being played was a 3 year old boy who stopped to listen. His mother, however, was in too much of a hurry and pulled her child away. The experiment proves that if we weren't so busy rushing around in modern life, we wouldn't miss out on the beauty around us so often. It also reminds us not to judge people by their appearance!

1. a. looks   b. purposes   c. senses   d. disappearances
2. a. with   b. out   c. on   d. over
3. a. mislead   b. misleading   c. misled   d. misleads
4. a. worthless   b. hopeless   c. meaningless   d. endless
5. a. majority   b. main   c. most   d. major
6. a. to   b. of   c. by   d. with
7. a. knew   b. has known   c. known   d. had known
8. a. approved   b. appreciated   c. desired   d. obeyed

C. Read the text and write T for True or F for False.

A world full of COLOUR

The natural world is extremely colourful with humans, plants and animals displaying many different shades of colour.

Human skin can be many different colours and it changes with the sun, our mood or our health for example. This is because of substances called 'pigments' which reflect light and make what the eye sees as colours. So, when we feel embarrassed, angry or upset for example, our heart can send more blood to the face and the pigments in the skin become red. This is why we have the expression that someone 'sees red' when they are angry.

Plants also have these pigments. Colour is very important for their survival. The bright colours and patterns of flowers draw the attention of insects which then carry their pollen from one flower to another, making sure the plants are reproduced. Bees can see colours we cannot, such as ultraviolet (UV), and they follow these to the inside of the flower. Without bees visiting flowers in this way, thousands of species of plants would not survive.

Animals also use colour for their own benefit. They protect themselves with different colours and patterns so as not to be seen by predators. The snowshoe hare for example, a type of wild rabbit, changes colour according to the time of year for this reason. During summer it is a brown colour, and in winter it is white so that it can hide in the snow. The chameleon, a type of lizard, changes colour instantly in order to protect itself. However, some animals use colour as a warning to scare away predators. Bright colours such as yellow, red and orange are often used in this way. These colours usually represent a negative aspect of the animal, like the bad taste of a monarch butterfly, the nasty smell of a skunk or the painful sting of a bee. Nature, however, is very clever, and predators also use colours to attract their prey. Also, many harmless creatures copy the colours of harmful ones to scare away predators by pretending to be dangerous.

So we can see that there may be as many different reasons and uses for colours in the natural world as there are different shades for the eye to see. Some uses of colour in nature remain a mystery, but one thing is for sure, colour does not only make our planet beautiful but it is also necessary for its survival.

1. The colour of our skin can change according to the way we are feeling.
2. Pigments are made from light from the sun.
3. The expression 'see red' comes from the fact that when we are angry more blood is sent to the eye.
4. Plants use bright colours to make themselves more attractive to certain insects.
5. Bees are a necessary part of plant reproduction.
6. Animals use bright colours such as red and yellow to hide from other animals.
7. Colours on animals can often mean that the creature has something nasty or poisonous.
8. All of the uses of colour in nature have been discovered.